curriculum
connections

21st Century Science

Chemistry

BROWN
BEAR
BOOKS

Published by Brown Bear Books Limited

An imprint of:
The Brown Reference Group Ltd
68 Topstone Road
Redding
Connecticut 06896
USA
www.brownreference.com

Editorial Director: Lindsey Lowe
Managing Editor: Tim Harris
Project Director: Paul Humphrey
Editor: Andrew Solway
Designer: Barry Dwyer
Picture Researcher: Andrew Solway

Library of Congress Cataloging-in-Publication Data available upon request

Picture Credits

Cover Image
Silicon wafers (Istockphoto, Hirkophooto)

Jupiter Images:
49 Photos.com; 63 liquidlibrary; 69 Photos.com

NASA:
20; 105 Goddard Space Flight Center Scientific Visualization Studio

Shutterstock:
7 Mikhail Pogosov; 17 Shutterstock; 26 Carolina K. Smith; 29 Ronald Caswell; 33 Olaf Rehmert; 35 Tim Mainiero; 43 Worldpics; 51 Hugo de Wolf; 56t Lisa F. Young; 56b Terry Reimink; 72 Noam Armonn; 74 Barskaya; 80 Bocos Benedict; 82 RTimages; 90 Shutterstock; 96 Roger Dale Pleis; 98 MichaelTaylor

Artwork © The Brown Reference Group Ltd

Printed in the United States of America

Contents

Introduction

21st Century Science forms part of the Curriculum Connections project. Between them, the six volumes of this set cover all the key disciplines of the science curriculum: Chemistry, The Universe, Living Organisms, Genetics, The Earth, and Energy and Matter.

In-depth articles form the core of each volume, and focus on the scientific fundamentals. Each article relates to those preceding it, and the most basic are covered early in each volume. However, each article may be studied independently. So, for example, the Chemistry book begins with some relatively basic articles on atoms and molecules before progressing to more complex topics. However, the student who already has a reasonable background knowledge can turn straight to the article about carbon-hydrogen compounds to gain a more thorough understanding.

Within each article there are two key aids to learning that are to be found in color bars located in the margins of each page:

Curriculum Context sidebars indicate to the reader that a subject has particular relevance to certain key State and National Science and Technology Education Standards up to Grade 12.

Glossary sidebars define key words within the text.

A summary Glossary lists the key terms defined in the volume, and the Index lists people and major topics covered.

Fully captioned illustrations play a major role in the set, including photographs, artwork reconstructions, and explanatory diagrams.

About this Volume

No region of modern science can be neatly detached from other fields; all are increasingly interrelated, and chemistry is no exception. It merges into ecology and biology on one side, physics on another, and earth sciences in other respects.

Elements combine into compounds when their atoms form chemical bonds with those of other elements, and compounds react by breaking some bonds and forming others. Chemical bonds themselves involve the exchange or sharing of electrons between atoms. Chemistry is essentially about the behavior of the atoms and electrons of the elements, and how they interact. About 30 million compounds are now known to scientists. Most are organic—that is, they contain carbon—but many are inorganic. Inorganic chemicals generally have no carbon in them, although they include a few carbon compounds such as the oxides of carbon and carbonate and bicarbonate salts.

Chemists need to be able to analyze substances to find out what they contain; to devise processes to create required substance cheaply and safely out of the available raw materials; and to predict the properties of a new compound before they go to the expense of creating it. Chemistry therefore combines the theoretical and the practical, the laboratory and the factory, in a unique way.

Chemistry combined with other sciences extends the possibilities for applying the chemist's knowledge. Biochemistry is increasingly important in medicine, and it contributes to the understanding of life itself. Physical and industrial chemistry are two other important areas of the discipline, and these, too, are covered in this volume.

Atoms and Elements

Chemists have always worked with atoms. The study of what happens between atoms during chemical changes is the basis of their science. Yet it was not until the invention of the scanning tunneling microscope in the 1980s that chemists were actually able to see atoms for the first time.

The ancient Greeks believed that atoms were particles that cannot be subdivided further, and named them "atomos" (indivisible).

We now know that atoms are made up of even smaller particles: protons, which carry a positive electrical charge; electrons, which have a negative electrical charge; and neutrons, which are neutral. The center, or nucleus, of most atoms is made up of neutrons and protons, and carries a positive charge. The electrons move around the nucleus in a series of "shells," or orbitals, held in place by the attraction of the positive charge of the protons in the nucleus.

Elements
Elements are substances that consist of only one type of atom, and cannot be broken down into a simpler substance. Because atoms are the smallest unit of a chemical element that retain the characteristics of the element, they are the building blocks of all things. Everything around us is made up of combinations of chemical elements.

It might seem impossible to predict the chemical and physical properties of an element without carrying out experiments. But because of the way that atoms interact with each other, it is only necessary to know the number of protons in the nucleus of the atom of that element—referred to as the atomic number—to predict quite a lot about an element's physical and chemical properties. The great predictive tool is a chart known as the Periodic Table.

The Periodic Table

In the Periodic Table, elements are arranged in order of increasing atomic number. Elements with similar physical and chemical properties are found at definite intervals, or periods, of atomic number. This periodicity makes it possible to predict the characteristics of an element simply by knowing its position in the table. When the Periodic Table was first compiled, periodicity made it possible for chemists to predict the existence of elements such as germanium (Ge), which were not then known.

Metals make up most of the elements and take up all of the left-hand side of the Periodic Table. The nonmetals appear on the right, separated from the metals by the metalloids.

The Group I elements, or alkali metals, react vigorously in water to create strong alkaline solutions. Group II elements, the alkaline earth metals, occur only as compounds in minerals that form rocks. The transition metals, which are usually divided into three blocks and occur between Groups II and III, are hard, tough, and

Atomic number

The number of protons in the nucleus of an element. Carbon, for instance, has 12 protons in its nucleus (atomic number = 12).

Curriculum Context

Students should know how to use the Periodic Table to identify metals, semi-metals, nonmetals, and halogens.

Russian chemist Dmitri Mendeleev was the first to organize the elements into the Periodic Table, in 1869. He was confident enough to leave spaces in his arrangement where no element fitted properly. Later, new elements were discovered that filled these gaps.

Curriculum Context

Students should know how to use the Periodic Table to identify alkali metals, alkaline earth metals, and transition metals.

shiny. Aluminum (Al), the third most abundant element on Earth, occurs in Group III. Carbon (C) and silicon (Si), equal second most abundant, are in Group IV. Group V elements include nitrogen (N) and phosphorus (P). Oxygen (O), the most abundant element on Earth, is in Group VI, along with sulfur (S). The Group VII elements, or halogens, are nonmetals and are so reactive that they are usually found combined with other elements in salts. The Group VIII elements, the noble or inert gases, are very different. Their outer electron shells are full, which makes them almost totally nonreactive.

So far, 117 elements have been discovered, named, and listed in the Periodic Table. Only 92 of these occur naturally. The others have been made synthetically in

The Periodic Table groups elements according to their physical and chemical properties. The elements are ordered by their atomic number. This appears at the top right of the element's square. The horizontal rows in the table are known as periods. From left to right, each element has one more electron in its outer shell than the last. Vertical columns on the table are known as groups. Elements in the same group all have the same number of electrons in their outer shell, and, as a result, they tend to have similar chemical properties.

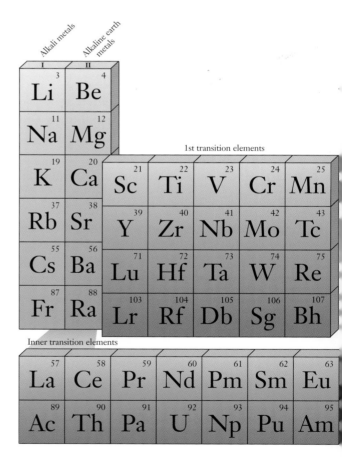

nuclear reactors and particle accelerators. Element 118, ununoctium, is the heaviest yet made. Element 117, ununseptium, has not yet been synthesized.

Isotopes

Isotopes are atoms of the same element that have different numbers of neutrons in their nuclei, although the number of protons remains the same. The total mass of neutrons and protons in an atom is known as its atomic mass. For convenience, chemists often refer to the relative atomic mass of an element (formerly known as atomic weight). This is found by comparing the mass of an "average" atom of an element, taking into account the proportions of all its isotopes, with a reference value equivalent to one-twelfth of the mass of an atom of carbon-12, an isotope of carbon.

	Halogens	Hydrogen	Noble gases

Boron group	Carbon group	Nitrogen group	Oxygen group			
					1 H	2 He
III	IV	V	VI	VII		VIII
5 B	6 C	7 N	8 O	9 F		10 Ne
13 Al	14 Si	15 P	16 S	17 Cl		18 Ar

2nd transition elements   3rd transition elements

26 Fe	27 Co	28 Ni	29 Cu	30 Zn	31 Ga	32 Ge	33 As	34 Se	35 Br	36 Kr
44 Ru	45 Rh	46 Pd	47 Ag	48 Cd	49 In	50 Sn	51 Sb	52 Te	53 I	54 Xe
76 Os	77 Ir	78 Pt	79 Au	80 Hg	81 Tl	82 Pb	83 Bi	84 Po	85 At	86 Rn
108 Hs	109 Mt	110 Ds	111 Rg	112 Uub	113 Uut	114 Uuq	115 Uup	116 Uuh	117 Uus	118 Uuo

64 Gd	65 Tb	66 Dy	67 Ho	68 Er	69 Tm	70 Yb
96 Cm	97 Bk	98 Cf	99 Es	100 Fm	101 Md	102 No

Mixtures, Compounds, and Solutions

When two or more atoms bond together, they form a molecule. Molecules can be made up of several atoms of the same element, or of atoms of different elements. They can come together in many ways to produce mixtures, solutions, emulsions, and compounds; all of these are important to the chemist, although compounds are what people think of as the special province of the chemist.

Curriculum Context

Students should know that atoms combine to form molecules by sharing electrons to form covalent or metallic bonds, or by exchanging electrons to form ionic bonds.

Solvent

A liquid in which certain solids or liquids dissolve.

Solute

A solid or liquid dissolved in a solvent.

Mixtures and compounds

An everyday example of a mixture can be found in a typical trash can. It probably contains a variety of different substances, such as glass, paper, plastic, and metal, all mixed together. In the trash can, no chemical reactions take place and the different components of the waste are mixed up but not bonded together chemically. It is an easy—if unpleasant—task to separate the different components physically, by characteristics such as size, texture, color, and density.

A cup of coffee or tea contains examples of both compounds and solutions. Compounds are molecules that contain atoms from at least two different elements. Water (H_2O) is the commonest and most abundant compound on Earth. In water, as in all compounds, the atoms are held together by chemical bonds. There are several kinds of chemical bond. These bonds involve either the sharing of electrons between atoms, or the transfer of one or more electrons from one atom to another. For such a bond to form or be broken a chemical reaction must take place, and the individual elements cannot be joined or separated by physical means such as shaking, pressing, or filtering.

Solvents and solutes

The molecular structure of water makes it an excellent solvent, and water is often known as the universal solvent because so many substances can be dissolved in it. The solvent action of water is essential for making a hot beverage such as coffee or tea. Hot water is used as a solvent to dissolve the flavorful juices from the ground coffee beans or the tea leaves. Some people also dissolve a solid solute (sugar) and a liquid solute (milk or cream) in the drink. These solutes are readily soluble in water. In solution they are broken down into molecules or ions, which become evenly dispersed throughout the solvent. The solute molecules will disperse through the hot drink without any help, but they dissolve more quickly if the drink is stirred. As well as the dissolved molecules, a cup of coffee contains tiny particles of the ground beans held in suspension, but these are not chemically altered as are the solutes. In hard water areas where the water contains calcium, magnesium, and bicarbonate ions, a film or scum may appear on the drink; this can be avoided by adding a weak acid such as lemon juice, instead of milk.

Ion
An atom that is positively or negatively charged.

Suspension
A mixture of fine solid particles in a liquid, in which the solid particles remain suspended in the liquid rather than precipitating (sinking to the bottom).

Emulsions

Margarine is a common example of an emulsion—a mixture of two liquids that do not dissolve in each other. In an emulsion, the components are not broken down—instead, tiny droplets of one liquid are suspended in the other. Margarine is an emulsion of milk (which is mainly water), fats, and oils. Normally oil and water do not mix, because the differences in their molecular structure mean that they have a stronger

Iron and Sulfur

Iron and sulfur are examples of elements. They cannot be broken down into simpler substances. If iron filings and powdered yellow sulfur are mixed together no chemical reaction occurs. The two components of the mixture can be separated relatively easily by using a magnet to remove the iron filings. But if the iron/sulfur mixture is heated, a chemical reaction does occur, and the two components can no longer be readily separated. When heated, the iron and sulfur react together to form a compound known as iron sulfide (FeS).

Salt and Water

Water is a very common but unusual compound held together by a weak hydrogen bond. Although made up of two gases, hydrogen and oxygen, water at room temperature is a liquid rather than a gas. Sodium chloride (NaCl), or common salt, is a compound made up of sodium and chlorine atoms. The sodium (Na) atoms have a positive charge, and the chlorine atoms (Cl) have a negative charge: they are both ions, held together by ionic bonds. NaCl dissolves readily in water. Once dissolved it splits into its component ions, which become surrounded by water molecules. The negatively charged Cl⁻ and positively charged Na⁺ ions are attracted to different ends of the water molecules. When the water is removed, the Na and Cl recombine to form salt crystals.

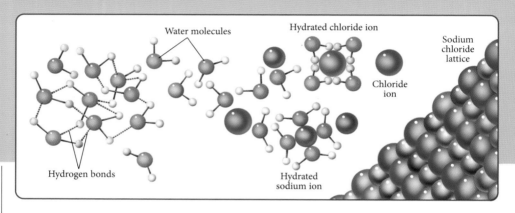

Water molecules

Hydrated chloride ion

Sodium chloride lattice

Chloride ion

Hydrogen bonds

Hydrated sodium ion

Curriculum Context

Students should know how to describe the dissolving process at the molecular level by using the concept of random molecular motion.

attraction for their own kind of molecule than for each other. It is possible to overcome this problem by shaking the mixture vigorously. Thus, when making a salad dressing the oil can be emulsified with vinegar, which is also mostly water. The shaking breaks up the two liquids into tiny droplets and causes them to form a temporary emulsion. When the droplets join together again, the two liquids soon separate, with the oil floating on top of the vinegar.

In margarine, a more permanent emulsion is required, so an emulsifier is used. Emulsifiers are molecules that contain one end that is attracted to oil and one end that is attracted to water. The natural emulsifier lecithin, which is found in egg yolks, is often used for emulsifying margarine.

Types of Bonds

Electrons are the smallest atomic particles—they are more than 1,800 times smaller than neutrons or protons—but they determine the chemical properties of atoms. Electrons are largely responsible for the way that atoms react, or bond, with other atoms.

Atoms join together to form a molecule when the pull of the nucleus of a nearby atom is stronger than the pull of their own nucleus, and electrons move to the outer shell of the neighboring atom, or become shared between two atoms. Understanding the role of electrons in bonding provides the key to understanding chemical reactions.

How atoms join

Atoms are always seeking chemical stability. Those that have an incomplete outer shell of electrons try to join up chemically with other atoms. In contrast, elements that have a full outer shell of electrons are very stable. Some examples of highly stable elements are the noble gases, such as neon and argon.

Atoms join together to form molecules and ionic compounds by means of chemical bonds. A chemical reaction, which involves the making or breaking of bonds, occurs spontaneously only if the products are more stable than the atoms that react. In bonding, atoms either lose, gain, or share electrons. The number of electrons that an atom has available to participate in bonding (usually the electrons in its outer shell) is known as its valence, or combining power.

Isomers

Atoms can combine in many ways. As a result, two compounds with the same chemical composition may have different forms, or isomers, which can also have different chemical properties. Understanding the properties of isomers is crucial in oil refining, for

Noble gases

Gases in Group VIII of the Periodic Table, all of . which are chemically unreactive.

example. To produce an automobile fuel with the optimum volatility (to make the car easy to start from cold) and the right octane number (so the car runs smoothly and with enough power), refiners must achieve the right balance of straight-chain and branched isomers of alkanes, the chief components in crude oil. Although both isomers have the same chemical composition, their molecular shapes are different, and as a result they perform differently as fuels. A fuel with too many straight-chain alkanes would be too volatile, and a fuel without enough branched alkanes would have a very low octane rating.

Chemical bonding

There are three main types of bond: ionic, metallic, and covalent. When an atom loses or gains electrons it becomes electrically charged, and is known as an ion. An ionic bond is formed when ions with opposite charges are held together by electrostatic attraction, and form a regular array, or crystal, also known as an ionic lattice. In common salt (NaCl) the sodium atoms lose an electron and take on a positive charge (Na^+), while the chlorine atoms gain an electron to take on a negative charge (Cl^-).

An ionic bond is formed when ions (charged atoms) with opposite charges are held together by electrostatic attraction. In common salt (NaCl), sodium atoms lose an electron to become positive ions, while chlorine atoms gain an electron to become negative ions.

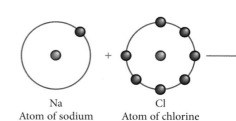

Na
Atom of sodium

Cl
Atom of chlorine

In covalent bonding, atoms do not gain or lose electrons; instead, they share their electrons with another atom. Electrons in covalent bonds are not always shared equally between the bonded elements. Where the sharing is unequal, as in a molecule of water (H_2O), the bond is known as a polar bond, and the resulting molecule has both a negatively and a positively charged end.

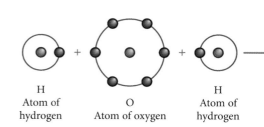

H
Atom of hydrogen

O
Atom of oxygen

H
Atom of hydrogen

In metallic bonding, a lattice is formed when all the metal atoms share their outer electrons to form a sea of electrons. Metallic bonds are very strong, and thus metals tend to have high melting and boiling points. In the metallic lattice the electrons can move freely, and this explains why metals are such good conductors of electricity and heat.

In covalent bonding, atoms do not gain or lose electrons; instead, they share their electrons. When only one electron is shared between the atoms—as, for example, in the fluorine molecule (F_2)—a single covalent bond is formed. When two electrons are shared, as in carbon dioxide (CO_2), the resulting covalent bond is known as a double bond. In acetylene (ethyne) (C_2H_2), where the two carbon atoms are held together by a triple bond, three electrons are shared.

Electrons in covalent bonds are not always shared equally between the bonded elements. Where the sharing is unequal, as in a molecule of water (H_2O), the bond is known as a polar bond, and the resulting molecule has both a negatively and a positively charged end.

Curriculum Context

Students should be aware that chemical bonds between atoms in molecules such as H_2, CH_4, NH_3, C_2H_2, N_2, Cl_2, and in many large biological molecules, are covalent.

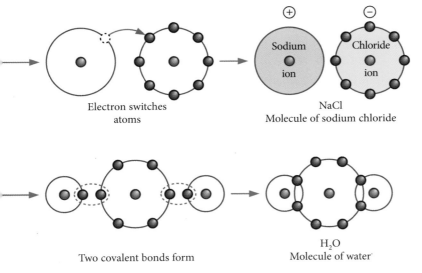

Electron switches
atoms

NaCl
Molecule of sodium chloride

Two covalent bonds form

H_2O
Molecule of water

Bonds and Structures

When two oxygen atoms join with one carbon atom by means of double covalent bonds, they form the relatively harmless gas carbon dioxide (CO_2). But when the same elements are bonded together in carbon monoxide (CO), the result is very different: lone pair electrons allow the carbon monoxide to bond as a ligand to other substances, and the compound is a poisonous gas that can kill.

Ligand

A substance that can form a complex in which a number of ligand molecules bond to a central atom, often a metal.

Amorphous

Having no regular structure.

Buckminster Fuller

American architect and inventor who invented the geodesic dome— a hemispherical structure built from flat five- and six-sided panels.

Physical properties

A chemical formula alone is not a reliable indicator of how a substance looks or what its physical properties are. These properties are greatly influenced by the way in which its molecules are attracted to one another. The stronger the attractive bonds, the higher the melting and boiling point of the substance.

Carbon illustrates how different kinds of bonding can affect the physical properties of a substance. Carbon exists naturally in four forms, or allotropes: amorphous carbon, graphite, diamond, and buckminsterfullerene. Amorphous carbon occurs in the soot formed during incomplete burning of hydrocarbon fuels, and consists of shapeless particles of carbon. In graphite, the carbon is arranged in thin sheets composed of a network of six-sided carbon rings. In diamond, the strongest form of carbon, every carbon atom is bonded to four others in a three-dimensional lattice. Buckminsterfullerene (C_{60}), the fourth allotrope of carbon, was first synthesized in 1985. Its basic structure consists of five- and six-sided carbon rings arranged like the panels of a soccer ball to make a sphere. It is named after American architect and inventor Buckminster Fuller.

Dipole attraction

Some molecules, such as water, are held together by polar covalent bonds, in which the electrons are shared unequally. This results in a dipole—a slight positive electrical charge at one end of the molecule and a slight negative charge at the other. These opposite charges attract and pull the molecules together. Hydrogen bonds are a very strong form of dipole–dipole attraction. Although they are weak compared with normal chemical bonds, they have some significant effects. Hydrogen bonding in water is responsible for its high surface tension. This is why some insects can walk on water. Hydrogen bonding also accounts for the relatively high boiling point of water. Energy (heat) is needed to break the hydrogen bonds and separate the liquid molecules into the free individual molecules found in a vapor.

Intermolecular forces do not have to be strong in order to be powerful. Van der Waals' forces, the "flickerings" of positive and negative charges that occur on the surface of molecules due to the constantly shifting position of the electrons, pull nonpolar molecules together, if no stronger force gets in the way. In graphite, for instance, covalent bonds hold together the carbon sheets themselves, but van der Waals' forces hold the layers together. The weak van der Waals' forces allow the layers to slide over each other. This is why graphite is such a good lubricant.

Curriculum Context

For many curricula, students should know how to identify solids and liquids held together by van der Waals' forces or hydrogen bonds, and be able to relate these forces to volatility and boiling/melting point temperatures.

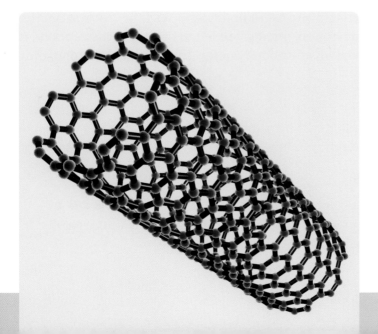

Carbon nanotubes are another form of carbon, derived from buckminsterfullerene. These tubelike molecules have many possible uses, ranging from extremely strong, lightweight materials to incredibly small electronic circuits and solar cells that are twice as efficient as the best conventional cells.

Chemical Reactions

The art of the chemist lies in understanding and controlling the chemistry that causes chemical reactions. Chemical reactions may take place either explosively or gradually, and some may not take place at all without help.

Reactant

An element or compound taking part in a chemical reaction.

The rate at which a reaction will take place, or whether it will occur at all, is determined by the types of reactants. In general terms atoms seek stability, which means having a complete outer shell of electrons. An element with just one electron in its outer shell, such as sodium, easily donates that electron. Hydrogen (which has only one electron in total) is also a good electron donor. It forms many compounds, including water, acids and bases, and many organic molecules. In contrast, halogens such as chlorine, which need only one electron to complete the outer shell, easily capture an electron. Elements such as sodium and chlorine can be so reactive that they are difficult to control.

Activation energy

In all chemical reactions, bonds are broken, made, or rearranged. During this process, energy—such as heat—is either taken in or given out. All reactions need some energy, known as the activation energy, to stretch and break bonds, and start the reaction off. The amount of energy needed to break a particular bond is known as its bond energy. The stronger the bond, the

Catalysts

Increasing temperature, pressure, or concentration can provide the activation energy needed to start off a reaction and increase its rate. Another way to do this is to use a catalyst. Catalysts are substances that speed up the rate of a reaction without undergoing any permanent chemical change themselves. The correct catalyst can accelerate very slow reactions, and make even very unreactive elements join together to form compounds.

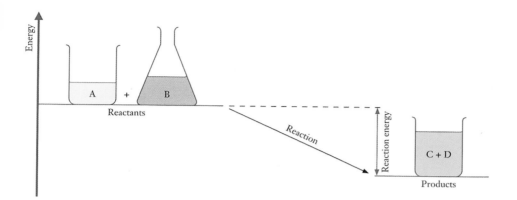

more difficult it is to break, and therefore the higher the bond energy is.

Endothermic and exothermic processes

Reactions such as cell respiration, acid/base neutralization, and combustion (for example, the burning of a campfire or a fireworks display) produce heat or release energy. These are known as exothermic reactions. Reactions such as photosynthesis (the reaction sequence by which plants convert the energy of sunlight into food) and electrolysis (a process used to electroplate or to purify metals) need a net input of energy to make them go forward. These types of reactions are known as endothermic reactions.

When an acid mixes with a base (an exothermic reaction), the heat that is produced is called the heat of neutralization. Mixing equivalent weights of sodium hydroxide and dilute hydrochloric or nitric acids, for example, yields about 13,550 calories of heat energy. Just adding concentrated sulfuric acid to water—in itself a dangerous procedure—generates heat as the acid dissolves. But most substances require heat to make them dissolve: the so-called endothermic heat of solution. That is why much more sugar or salt will dissolve in hot water than in cold water. The opposite is

The energy evolved when substances A and B (the reactants) combine to form C and D (the products) is called the reaction energy. Generally, this takes the form of heat. Usually, some activation is required before A and B will react together to form C and D.

The main tank of the Space Shuttle *Discovery* contains tanks of liquid hydrogen and liquid oxygen. Hydrogen, the fuel, is burned in oxygen, the oxidizer, producing huge amounts of heat and light. This exothermic reaction provides the power for lift-off.

also true—some substances yield heat (called the heat of crystallization) when they crystallize out of solution.

As long ago as 1874, the science-fiction writer Jules Verne predicted that the hydrogen and oxygen in water would one day be employed as a fuel. In fact, reactions between oxygen and hydrogen—the two components of water—are sometimes highly exothermic. A mixture of oxygen and hydrogen gas can be highly explosive. The energy given off during the exothermic reaction that occurs when hydrogen is burned in oxygen provides the power for lift-off of spacecraft such as the US Space Shuttle.

Liquid oxygen alone is used as the oxidizer in some rocket fuels. Alternatively, the oxidizing agent, which enables the fuel to burn, can be another gas such as fluorine or nitrogen dioxide; a liquid containing oxygen, such as hydrogen peroxide; or a solid containing oxygen, such as potassium nitrate.

Names and Formulas

To be useful to chemists, chemical names should indicate the composition of a compound, as well as give structural information about the shape and the nature of the chemical bonds. But for consumers, an easy-to-remember trade name, which we can associate with a known product that performs a specific job, is sufficient. Many of these names do contain some chemical information and have become household words.

IUPAC names

Although a number of systems for naming chemical compounds have been developed in the past, the majority of chemists now rely on a form of systematic nomenclature supported by the International Union of Pure and Applied Chemistry (IUPAC). In this system, the name of a compound describes various important characteristics, such as the types of cyclic compounds or functional groups the molecule contains, and what sort of bonding holds it together. The great advantage of the IUPAC system is that chemists throughout the world can understand something about the structure and chemistry of an organic compound just by knowing its name. The disadvantage is that sometimes the names are very complicated. For example, glucose (a sugar) is referred to as 1,3,4,5,6–pentahydroxy-hexanal under the IUPAC system.

Compounds can also be represented by chemical formulas, which show what elements are present in the compound and in what proportion. An example familiar even to most people outside the scientific community is the chemical formula for water, H_2O, which indicates a compound made of two atoms of hydrogen and one of oxygen.

Chemical equations offer a simple way to describe the changes that take place during chemical reactions. The

Nomenclature

Any system devised for giving things names.

Functional group

A chemically reactive group of atoms, such as an alcohol (OH) or amine (NH3) group, in an organic (carbon-based) compound.

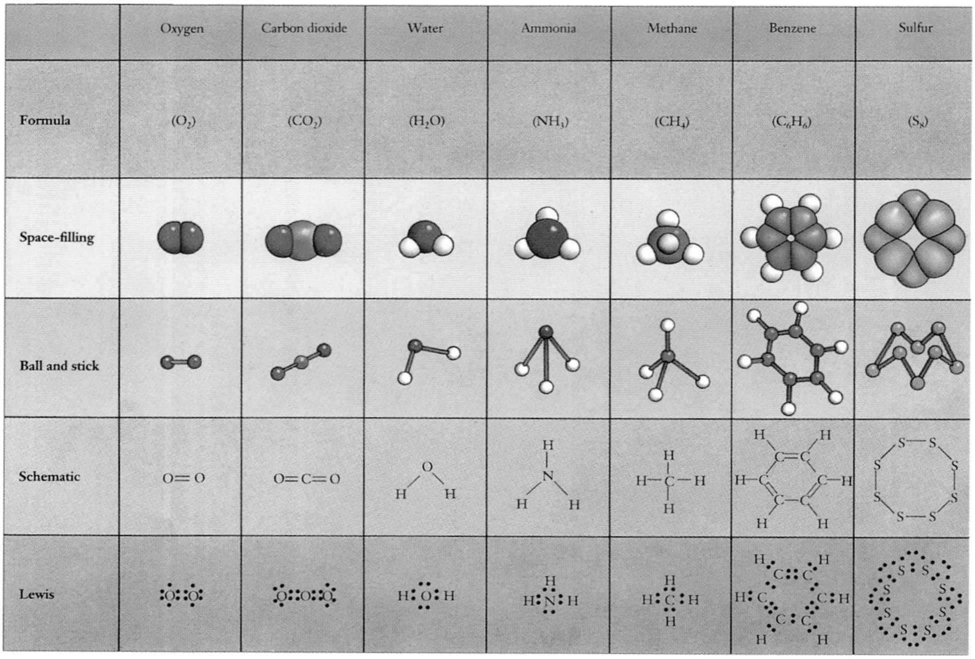

	Oxygen	Carbon dioxide	Water	Ammonia	Methane	Benzene	Sulfur
Formula	(O_2)	(CO_2)	(H_2O)	(NH_3)	(CH_4)	(C_6H_6)	(S_8)
Space-filling							
Ball and stick							
Schematic	O=O	O=C=O	H—O—H (bent)	N with three H	H—C—H with H above and below	benzene ring C=C	S ring S—S
Lewis	:O::O:	:O::O::O:	H:O:H	H:N:H with H	H:C:H with H	benzene Lewis ring	S ring Lewis

Some conventions for illustrating the structure of molecules. In space-filling diagrams, atoms are drawn as spheres in proportion to their relative sizes. In simple structural diagrams, bonds are represented by straight lines. Lewis diagrams use dots to indicate the number of valence electrons of an atom. They are very useful for representing covalent bonds.

number of atoms of the reactants are shown on the left-hand side of the equation. The number of atoms of the products are shown on the right-hand side. Because no atoms are either created or lost during a chemical reaction, chemical equations are balanced, so that the total number of atoms of each element on the left is equal to the total number of each on the right.

Balanced equations give a good deal of information about what compounds are made from and how they form, but they do not indicate how quickly the reactions take place. The speed of a reaction can be affected by changing the temperature or pressure under which it takes place.

Acids, Bases, and Salts

Indigestion tablets use acid–base chemistry to soothe the stomach. The tablets commonly contain bases, which neutralize some of the acid present in the stomach. This eases the symptoms of indigestion, which is due to excess acid in the stomach.

What are acids and bases?

Acids are compounds that contain hydrogen and dissolve in water to release hydrogen ions. Because a hydrogen ion is a hydrogen atom that has lost its electron and therefore consists of just one proton, acids are also known as proton donors. When they are dissolved in water, acids act as electrolytes.

The strongest acids are highly corrosive substances, and accordingly they must be handled with great care. Other acids, such as vinegar and citric acid, are much less corrosive. They can be used to add flavor to foods with their sour, sharp taste.

The protons in acids are readily accepted by bases. Bases are good proton acceptors because they often contain oxide (O^{--}) or hydroxide (OH^-) ions. Many bases cannot be dissolved in water. Those that can are known as alkalis. Indigestion tablets and cleaners for household drains are everyday bases. Industrial bases include caustic soda (sodium hydroxide, $NaOH$) and lime (calcium oxide, CaO).

Neutralization

When acids and bases are mixed, they combine in a reaction known as neutralization to form an ionic compound, called a salt, and water. For example, hydrochloric acid (HCl) neutralizes sodium hydroxide ($NaOH$) to produce common salt (sodium chloride, $NaCl$) and water (H_2O). Neutralization reactions of this kind are exothermic: heat is released into the surroundings as the reaction takes place.

Electrolyte

An ionic compound, such as an acid, alkali, or salt, which allows ions to flow through it. Electrolytes conduct electricity when they are melted or dissolved.

Curriculum Context

Students should know that acids are hydrogen-ion-donating and bases are hydrogen-ion-accepting substances. Many curricula ask students to compare and contrast the properties of acids and bases, to provide a context for understanding their behavior.

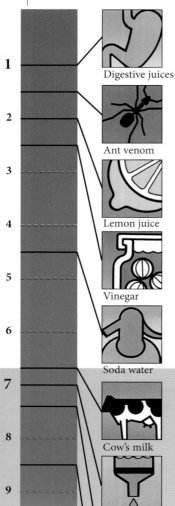

1 — Digestive juices
2 — Ant venom
3
4 — Lemon juice
5 — Vinegar
6 — Soda water
7
8 — Cow's milk
9 — Pure water
10
11 — Blood
12 — Toothpaste
13
14 — Washing soda

Acid and base strength

The concentration of an acid or base varies with the amount of water present in the solution. Strength is determined by the ability to dissociate, or split up into cations and anions. Weak acids and bases only partly dissociate. Strong acids and bases, which can dissociate completely into ions, have more proton donors or acceptors.

The strength of an acid or base can be measured by the concentration of hydrogen ions in a solution, known as the pH. Various pH values can be determined with an indicator, a substance whose color changes when the pH changes. Litmus indicators distinguish between acids, which turn them red, and bases, which turn them blue. Universal indicators change color according to the pH scale.

The pH Scale

The pH scale is used to specify the strength of an acid or a base. Neutral substances, such as milk, blood, and pure water, have pH values around 7.

Acids have pH values of less than 7. Lemon juice (pH 2.2) and vinegar (pH 3.0) are familiar acids in the kitchen. The "sting" in stinging nettles, and the stings of ants, are caused by formic acid (methanoic acid, $HCOOH$, pH 1.5). The acid in the stomach's digestive fluids (HCl), at pH 1, is one of the strongest acids.

Alkaline compounds have pH values greater than 7. Toothpastes are usually slightly alkaline; the base can serve to neutralize the acids formed in the mouth by the action of bacteria on food. Cleaners such as dishwashing detergent often contain alkalis, which act as grease removers.

Combustion and Fuel

Fuels are compounds that contain stored chemical energy. This energy, which is released by the making and breaking of bonds, is given off in the form of heat when the fuel is broken down. The heat, in turn, can be used to do work, or it can be converted into other forms of energy. Food is the fuel that animals rely on to provide energy to keep them alive. Hydrocarbons, such as oil, gas, and coal, are the fuels used to provide the energy to heat houses, run engines, and generate electricity. Different fuels release different amounts of energy.

Respiration and combustion

Respiration is the chemical process that happens within cells, by which animals get energy from their food. During respiration, organisms break down fuels such as glucose or other sugars with oxygen, to produce water (H_2O) and carbon dioxide (CO_2). The energy released as a result of this process is used to help the organism live and grow. In a similar way, fuels such as oil, natural gas, and coal release energy by combustion (burning) in air or oxygen to give out heat. During the combustion of hydrocarbon fuels, carbon and hydrogen react with oxygen and are oxidized to form carbon dioxide (CO_2) and water (H_2O).

The rate of combustion depends on conditions such as the concentration of oxygen. Air is only around one-fifth oxygen (the rest is mainly inert nitrogen), and fuels burn much faster in pure oxygen. Controlling the concentration of the fuel is also important for controlling combustion.

Just as the energy from a match is needed to light a candle, so energy—usually in the form of heat—is needed to start off the combustion reaction. This activation energy is used to break bonds, so that new bonds can start to form. Because the combustion

Hydrocarbon

A chemical compound that is made up only of carbon and hydrogen atoms. Fossil fuels are made up of hydrocarbons.

E85 is a biofuel that contains 85 per cent bioethanol (ethanol made from plant oils) and 15 per cent gasoline. Biofuels are plant-based fuels being developed as cleaner alternatives to fossil fuels, with much lower carbon emissions.

reaction is exothermic overall, it provides its own energy once the reaction gets going. As with a burning candle, the reaction stops only when the supply of fuel or oxygen runs out.

Energy from fuel

The amount of energy given off by the combustion of a fuel depends on the number of bonds to be broken and made. This factor is generally related to the size of the fuel molecule and the type of bonds involved. For this reason, larger hydrocarbon molecules such as hexane (C_6H_{14}), a typical constituent of gasoline, give off more energy per molecule than fuels such as methane (natural gas, CH_4), which has only a few carbon atoms. Partly oxidized fuels—including ethanol (C_2H_5OH), the alcohol in alcoholic drinks—are used as alternatives to petrol in some countries, but they give off even less energy. This is because they already contain O–H bonds in their structure. Because the energy released during combustion comes from the making of bonds to oxygen, fuels that already contain oxygen give out less energy when they burn. A compromise being tested in some countries is a fuel that is a combination of an alcohol—methanol or ethanol—and conventional gasoline (petrol).

Greener fuels

Power is not the only factor to consider when choosing a fuel. The use of alcohol-containing fuels in cars can help to reduce atmospheric pollution because they burn more completely than hydrocarbons, and give off lower amounts of carbon monoxide (CO), sulfur dioxide (SO_2), and nitrogen oxides (NOx) when they burn. It is these compounds that combine with water in the atmosphere to form acid rain, and contribute to photochemical smog at or near ground level. The oldest fuel of all—coal or coke—is a major cause of pollution, because its main combustion product is the greenhouse gas carbon dioxide.

Ignition points

Fuels differ in other ways besides the amounts of energy they give off when they burn. Different fuels also have different boiling points and flash, or ignition, points. These properties are related to their individual molecular structure, especially the number of carbon atoms they contain. Gasoline, with between 5 and 10 carbon atoms in its structure, has a low flash point. It ignites at any temperature above about 1.5°F (–17°C). This is a useful characteristic when it comes to starting a car in cold weather. The fuel oil used in domestic furnaces, on the other hand, which contains between 20 and 30 carbon atoms per molecule, has a flash point of around 126°F (52°C). However, once fuel oil begins to burn, gives off larger amounts of heat per gallon of fuel than gasoline does.

Ignition point
The temperature at which a fuel will begin to burn.

Controlling Fire

Understanding the chemical reactions that occur during fires can make it possible to keep a fire under control, or to prevent it in the first place. Fire requires fuel, oxygen, and heat. These three elements are often known as the fire triangle. Like all exothermic reactions, fires need energy to begin. Liquid fuel ignites only when it has reached its flash point. Once burning, the fire produces heat to keep the reaction going. But if the fuel or the oxygen is removed, the fire will go out.

Fire extinguishers are designed to put out fires by attacking one or more sides of the fire triangle. There are many different types of extinguishers. The chemical and physical nature of the fuel, as well as the size of the fire, are important things to consider when deciding which to use. Water is used to put out many types of fire. It works by cooling the fire and thus breaking the heat side of the fire triangle. However, water cannot be used on electrical fires, and a stream of water directed at an oil fire serves only to disperse the oil and thus spread the fire. Some firefighting methods attempt to break two sides of the fire triangle by combining the use of water, which cools the fire, with foams, which form a heavy blanket to exclude oxygen.

Carbon dioxide
Carbon dioxide (CO_2) is often used in water-based fire extinguishers to spray the water, but on its own it is a very effective extinguisher for all confined fires. In carbon dioxide extinguishers, liquid CO_2 stored under pressure becomes a heavier-than-air gas when released, and acts as an inert blanket to exclude oxygen from the fire.

Dry chemical extinguishers
Exclusion of oxygen, along with a cooling effect, is also the main action in dry chemical extinguishers, which

are often used to extinguish small electrical fires. In these extinguishers, a dry powder, made up principally of sodium hydrogen carbonate (sodium bicarbonate, $NaHCO_3$), decomposes when heated to produce CO_2. As in other CO_2 extinguishers, the CO_2 gas acts to exclude oxygen, and because the reaction is driven by the heat of the fire, the CO_2 is produced exactly where it is needed. The powder itself helps to blanket and cool the fire and reduces access for air.

Firefighters are often shown outside buildings pointing their hoses upward, but this is a misleading image. Firefighters usually train their hoses on the base of a fire, because this is more effective. And where possible they now try to fight fires from inside a building, rather than from the outside.

Halogenated hydrocarbons

Halogenated hydrocarbons, such as tetrachloro-methane (carbon tetrachloride, CCl_4), used in some chemical fire extinguishers, have an even greater smothering effect. They are more than three times as dense as CO_2, and so provide a highly effective blanket of vapor to cut off the oxygen supply. However, they must be used with care: CCl_4 decomposes to the highly toxic gas carbonyl chloride (phosgene, $COCl_2$). For this reason the use of CCl_4 extinguishers is forbidden in some places. Bromofluorocarbons have also been used in extinguishers, but are now being phased out because they are sources of bromine atoms, which deplete the Earth's ozone layer.

Larger fires

Fire extinguishers can be useful as "fire first aid" for putting out small fires before they become dangerous. Larger fires require more than the topical application of chemicals to douse the flames. Local fire departments and other organizations often conduct short courses in fire prevention as well as in the proper and effective use of fire extinguishers.

Very large fires such as forest or bush fires require more than the use of extinguishers or hoses to put them out. Hoses can be used to try and control the flames, while bulldozers create fire breaks (areas of bare ground), which stop the spread of the fire by removing its fuel. Aircraft and helicopters spraying water or chemical extinguishers from above can also help to douse the flames. However, in conditions such as hot weather and strong winds after a long dry season, such fires can be almost impossible to put out completely. Sometimes it is only a change in the wind or a rainstorm that eventually stops the fire.

Ozone layer

A thin layer in the upper atmosphere that is rich in a variant form of oxygen (O_3) known as ozone. The ozone layer protects the Earth from harmful utraviolet and other radiation.

Chemical Explosives

An explosion is the dramatic result when an exothermic (energy-producing) reaction releases energy faster than the energy can dissipate into the surroundings, with the production of large volumes of gases. The energy given off during the reaction causes the temperature to rise, the gases to expand, and the reaction rate to increase. If the reaction accelerates quickly enough to generate a pressure wave, an explosion takes place.

Gunpowder

The controlled chemical explosives used today depend on combustion reactions involving oxygen and a fuel. So did the earliest explosive—gunpowder. It was invented in China soon after the year 1000, and used at first to make firecrackers for livening up parades and celebrations. Later it was used as a propellant explosive, initially to fire arrows from bamboo tubes, and then by the year 1200 in rockets.

Gunpowder was introduced from the east or invented independently in Europe in about 1240, some say by the English scholar Roger Bacon (*ca.* 1214–1296). This explosive, also known as black powder from its color, consists of a finely ground mixture of carbon (charcoal), sulfur, and potassium nitrate (saltpeter). The carbon and sulfur are fuels, and the potassium nitrate is an oxidizer that produces oxygen when heated and enables the fuel to burn. The carbon and sulfur burn rapidly to produce the gases carbon dioxide and sulfur dioxide. It is the expansion of these gases that drives a gunpowder rocket, or forces a shell or bullet out of a gun barrel.

Nitroglycerin and dynamite

The first attempts to better gunpowder as an explosive used single substances that combined fuel and oxidizer in the same molecule, although such compounds tend

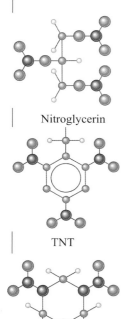

Nitroglycerin

TNT

RDX (cyclonite)

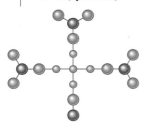

PETN

Many explosives contain several nitro groups (NO_2). Nitrocellulose was one of the first explosives discovered after gunpowder. TNT is one of the most powerful known explosives. RDX and PETN are used to make plastic explosives.

to be dangerously unstable. One of these molecules is nitroglycerin (chemical name glyceryl trinitrate), which has been used as an explosive since the mid-18th century. It is made by nitrating the syrupy liquid glycerol (glycerin) with a mixture of concentrated nitric and sulfuric acids. It is so sensitive that it cannot be handled safely by itself—it can only be used in combination with other materials, such as in dynamite.

Dynamite was invented by the Swedish engineer Alfred Nobel in an attempt to find a safe way of handling liquid nitroglycerin, after his brother was killed in an explosion at their factory in 1864. The nitroglycerin in dynamite is absorbed into a nonvolatile material such as the mineral kieselguhr (diatomaceous earth) or even wood pulp. Modern dynamite uses sodium nitrate to replace some of the nitroglycerin, making it even less dangerous to handle. And all forms of dynamite need a detonator to set them off—they cannot be exploded by hitting them with a hammer.

Nitrocellulose and TNT
Blasting gelatin, another form of high explosive, contains nitrocellulose. It is made by nitrating cellulose, usually obtained from wood pulp or cotton. One early form was known as guncotton. Nitrocellulose is best-known as a propellant explosive in cartridges for guns and small arms. It burns with a clear flame. The first successful version of this "smokeless powder" was called Cordite because it was manufactured in the form of long strands. When packed into a cartridge case and detonated, the explosive burns rapidly and evenly. TNT (trinitrotoluene) is one of the most powerful explosives. It is also based on a nitro compound, made by nitrating the coal-tar product toluene.

Detonators are highly sensitive explosives that explode when struck. Fulminates of heavy metals are typical compounds used as detonators; one example is

Fireworks make use of various explosives. Rockets have a relatively slow-burning propellant explosive to launch them into the air, and pellets of high explosives to make the bangs. Various chemicals—usually mineral salts—provide the color.

mercury fulminate, C=NOHg, made from the metal mercury, nitric acid, and ethanol. It was first employed in the early 1800s in percussion caps for muzzle-loading firearms. It was later used in Nobel's blasting caps for detonating dynamite.

Plastic explosives

Modern high explosives include ANFO (ammonium nitrate–fuel oil) mixtures. Ammonium nitrate can also be incorporated into a water-based gel or made into pellets called prills. All these products are used in mining, mostly in North America. Mixing a high explosive with wax and plasticizers produces plastic explosives, the best known being Semtex (named for Semt in the Czech Republic, where it was first made). The high explosive component in a plastic explosive is RDX (cyclonite), PETN (pentaerythritol tetranitrate), or a combination of the two. Plastic explosives are safe to handle, and can be molded to fit a cavity or wrap around a structure in demolition work.

Fulminate

A salt of fulminic acid (HCNO—an isomer of isocyanic acid).

Photochemistry

As we have seen, most chemical reactions require energy to make them start. Often this energy takes the form of heat, but some reactions are sparked by light. Light is a type of electromagnetic energy that travels as tiny "packets" called photons, whose energy depends on the wavelength of the light. When an atom or molecule absorbs a photon of light, it adopts a so-called excited state as its energy increases. It can then readily take part in reactions.

Some of the best known photochemical reactions take place in photography. The life-giving process of photosynthesis is another example of a photochemical reaction. This is described later, on pages 101–103. Other photochemical processes take place in the retina of the eye and are responsible for vision.

Reaction of chlorine and hydrogen

One of the first photochemical reactions to be studied in detail was the action of light on a dry mixture of chlorine and hydrogen gases. The final result of the reaction is the formation of hydrogen chloride, which occurs in a series of stages that make up a chemical chain reaction. First of all, in the initiation stage, light splits molecules of chlorine (Cl_2) into two chlorine atoms (Cl), each chlorine molecule absorbing one photon of light in the process. Then, in the propagation stage, each of the highly reactive chlorine atoms immediately reacts with a hydrogen molecule (H_2) to produce hydrogen chloride (HCl) and a free hydrogen atom (H). The free hydrogen atom reacts with another chlorine molecule to produce more hydrogen chloride and another free chlorine atom.

These second and third reactions repeat over and over again in what is termed a chain reaction. It may proceed so rapidly as to result in an explosion. The reaction comes to an end in the termination stage,

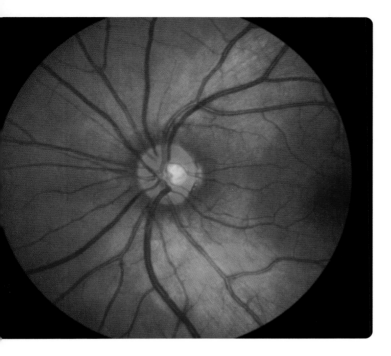

A view of the retina of the human eye through an ophthalmoscope. The cone cells (focused mainly at the center of the eye) perceive color but work only at high light levels. The rod cells (more numerous around the edges of the retina) do not perceive color, but operate in very low light levels.

when all chlorine and hydrogen atoms—the chain carriers—are eliminated because they have combined to form hydrogen chloride.

A similar light-induced chain reaction occurs between methane and chlorine. During initiation, light energy splits chlorine molecules into atoms. Propagation involves the production of methyl radicals (unstable, highly reactive forms of methane). During termination, the chlorine atoms and methane radicals combine in various ways to form chlorine (Cl_2), ethane (CH_3CH_3), and chloromethane (CH_3Cl).

Photography
Until the advent of digital cameras, photographic film was a common application of photochemistry. The film's emulsion (the light-sensitive coating on the film's surface) is made up of grains of a silver halide, usually silver bromide ($AgBr$). When a photograph is taken, the film is exposed to light for a fraction of a second. This causes some of the millions of molecules in each silver

Curriculum Context

For many curricula, students should know about radical reactions, in which chemical bonds are broken by heat or light to form highly reactive radicals. Radical reactions control processes such as ozone and greenhouse gas formation, and explosions.

halide grain to break down into silver and halide ions. The greater the exposure to light, the more molecules are broken down. Thus, areas of the film exposed to light-colored objects contain large numbers of silver atoms, but areas exposed to darker objects do not.

When the film is developed, the latent image is transformed into a picture by using a strong reducing agent, such as hydroquinone ($C_6H_4(OH)_2$), as a developer. The silver atoms in the areas of film exposed to light act as catalysts of a reaction in which the developer breaks down the silver halide into silver and halogen ions. The areas of the film exposed to dark objects have no silver atoms to act as a catalyst, so no silver halide is broken down. The result is a negative image in which black and white are reversed, because the silver halide is white, whereas the silver atoms appear black. Similar photochemical reactions are used to make an enlarged positive print from the negative.

The ozone layer

Very energetic light, such as ultraviolet (UV) light, can initiate photochemical reactions in the atmosphere and produce ozone, an allotrope of oxygen with the formula O_3. First, a photon of UV light splits an oxygen molecule (O_2) into two oxygen atoms (O). Then each oxygen atom combines with an oxygen molecule to form a molecule of ozone:

$$O + O_2 \rightarrow O_3$$

The result is a layer of ozone at a height of about 15 miles (25 km) in the stratosphere. The layer acts as a shield by blocking the passage of harmful UV radiation that would otherwise reach the Earth's surface. Ozone is also produced nearer the ground, where it forms part of photochemical smog.

Allotropy

The property that some elements have of being able to take two or more different structural forms. Graphite and diamond, for example, are two allotropes of carbon.

Curriculum Context

In many curricula, students should be aware that solar radiation ionizes atoms in the stratosphere and dissociates oxygen to form ozone, O_3. This process is important to life on Earth because ozone absorbs harmful ultraviolet radiation that would otherwise cause health problems.

A Cleaner Environment

When plants and bacteria convert, or "fix," nitrogen into soluble compounds, the result is increased productivity of the soil. But when cars fix nitrogen, the result is air pollution. Car exhaust combines with sulfur and other emissions from factory chimneys and power plants. The result is acid rain and a dangerous cocktail of airborne chemical pollution.

Industrial pollution

Air-polluting chemicals such as oxides of carbon, sulfur, and nitrogen are the byproducts of chemical industrial processes. Nitrogen oxides, along with sulfur oxides emitted from coal-fired power plants, are major causes of acid rain. Other emissions can lead to respiratory and skin problems for people who live near the plants. To cut down on emissions, plant operators can develop new processes that do not cause emissions in the first place, or they can devise ways of cleaning up the exhaust gases before they are released into the atmosphere. Most operators of factories choose the clean-up option.

For factory chimneys, flue gas desulfurization is the most common method for neutralizing acidic gases such as sulfur dioxide (SO_2). Typically, this process uses scrubbers—compartments inserted inside the chimney in which an alkali such as limestone reacts with the sulfur dioxide and removes it in the form of gypsum, which can then be used in other ways.

Curriculum Context

For most curricula, students should know that acids react with metal hydroxides, or bases, to produce water and a salt.

Vehicle pollutants

Cars, trucks, and buses are a far greater source of pollutants. Vehicle exhausts are responsible for most of the carbon monoxide (CO) released into the air. Vehicles also release nitrogen oxides, as well as unburned hydrocarbons. When nitrogen oxides react with unburned hydrocarbons, oxygen, and water vapor

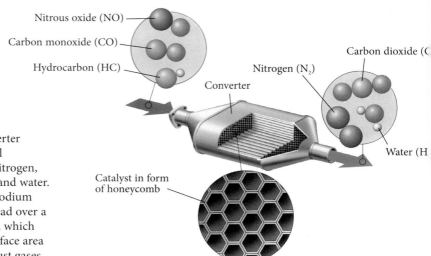

Nitrous oxide (NO)

Carbon monoxide (CO)

Hydrocarbon (HC)

Carbon dioxide (C

Nitrogen (N$_2$)

Converter

Water (H

Catalyst in form
of honeycomb

A catalytic converter
converts harmful
emissions into nitrogen,
carbon dioxide, and water.
Platinum and rhodium
catalysts are spread over a
ceramic support, which
increases the surface area
exposed to exhaust gases.

in the presence of sunlight, ozone is formed near the
ground. Ozone in the upper atmosphere protects the
Earth from harmful ultraviolet radiation, but at ground
level it damages many biological molecules, and results
in eye-irritating photochemical smogs.

Vehicle exhaust pollution is caused by the incomplete
combustion of fuel because there is insufficient
oxygen. Automotive engineers are currently
experimenting with "lean burn" engines, which use a
higher air-to-fuel ratio than normal in order to burn
fuel more completely.

Catalytic converters

The most efficient way to cut down on vehicle exhaust
emissions is to fit a three-way catalytic converter
between the engine and the tailpipe. Most modern
vehicles are fitted with such a converter. In the
converter, a catalyst such as powdered platinum and
rhodium is spread over a ceramic support. The catalyst
promotes chemical reactions that change carbon
monoxide, unburned hydrocarbons, and nitrogen
oxides into carbon dioxide (CO_2), water, and nitrogen,
by promoting the oxidation of carbon monoxide and
hydrocarbons, and the reduction of nitrogen oxides.

Catalyst

A substance that promotes
or accelerates a chemical
reaction without itself
being permanently
changed in the reaction.

Electricity and Chemistry

The addition and removal of electrons is one of the key processes in chemical bonding—and it is the basis of electrochemistry, in which electrical potentials are used to drive chemical reactions. Electrochemistry is used to make some important industrial chemicals. It is also used for electroplating, in medical applications, and in waste management.

Industrial electrochemistry

To industrial chemists, electrochemistry offers many advantages. For a start, it can be used to produce many products more cheaply, and with less harm to the environment. This is because the energy needed to drive electrochemical reactions comes largely from the electrical potential of the reactants. As a consequence, reactions can be run at lower temperatures, and energy costs are lower. In addition, because only the direct transfer of electrons is involved, many oxidation/reduction processes can be carried out without using harsh chemicals. Instead, electrons are supplied directly to the chemical reaction via electrodes dipped into the reaction mixture.

Electrochemical reactions are carried out in electrochemical cells. These contain an electrolyte; a power supply; a positive electrode (anode), which accepts electrons; and a negative electrode (cathode), which releases electrons. An electrochemical cell works in the opposite way to a battery. In a battery, electricity is produced by a chemical reaction (the movement of ions through an electrolyte from one type of metal electrode to another). In an electrochemical cell, electricity is used to drive a chemical reaction.

Electrochemistry is already used in a wide range of industrial processes. Electrolysis is used to manufacture many important chemicals. The electrolysis of brine, for

Electrolyte
An ionic compound, such as an acid, alkali, or salt, which allows ions to flow through it. Electrolytes conduct electricity when they are melted or dissolved.

Electrolysis
The process that occurs when an electrolyte conducts electricity.

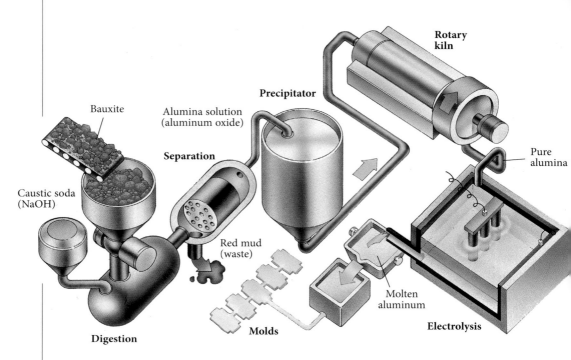

Bauxite

Alumina solution
(aluminum oxide)

Separation

Caustic soda
(NaOH)

Precipitator

Rotary
kiln

Pure
alumina

Red mud
(waste)

Molten
aluminum

Molds

Electrolysis

Digestion

A schematic diagram
showing the
processing of bauxite
and its electrolysis to
produce aluminum.

example, produces three industrial products: sodium
hydroxide (NaOH), chlorine, and hydrogen gas. The
method involves graphite anodes and a pool of liquid
mercury as a cathode; the electrolyte is brine, made up
of 25 percent salt (NaCl) dissolved in water. Chlorine
gas is given off at the graphite anodes. The sodium
atoms discharge at the negative mercury cathode,
where they form an amalgam with the mercury. This
amalgam flows out into another cell, where it is mixed
with water over activated carbon to remove the
sodium. The mercury flows back into the original cell,
while the sodium in the second cell reacts with the
water to produce sodium hydroxide solution and
hydrogen gas.

Metal refining

Electrolysis is also used to extract reactive metals, to
refine metals, and to anodize aluminum, giving it a
tougher surface. Aluminum is also usually extracted
from its main ore, bauxite, using electrolysis. In this
process, ore is dissolved (at a temperature of 1,832°F,
1,000°C) in molten cryolite, a naturally occurring

aluminum fluoride salt that acts as an electrolyte. Carbon is used for both the anodes and the cathodes. When an electric current is passed between the electrodes, positive aluminum ions collect at the negatively-charged cathode, where they form molten aluminum, which can be drained off. The process consumes large amounts of electricity, so it is economical only where a reliable supply of cheap electricity is available.

Curriculum Context

For most curricula, students need to know the common properties of salts, including the fact that most salts are soluble in water. When dissolved, they become conductors of electricity.

Electrolysis is also a useful method of purifying other metals, such as copper. Here, impure copper is used as the anode, and a sheet of pure copper is used as the cathode. The electrolyte is an acidified copper (II) sulfate solution ($CuSO_4$). During electrolysis the anode dissolves and the copper ions are deposited as pure copper on the cathode.

Electroplating

In electroplating, electrolysis is used to coat metals. The object to be plated is used as the cathode of the electrochemical cell, while the anode is made from the metal being used to plate the object.

New forms of electrochemistry

Chemists are beginning to exploit electrochemistry in new ways. In medicine, electrochemical cells can be used as biological monitoring devices, or biosensors, by adapting them to monitor a specific biological reaction. For example, a tiny glucose sensor has been developed that diabetic people can use to monitor their blood glucose levels.

Electrochemistry is also being explored as a means of removing pollutants from organic waste materials. The process involves using electrochemical processes to generate highly oxidizing metal ions and free radicals that react with waste molecules and turn them into harmless water and carbon dioxide.

The Chemical Industry

The chemical industry works to transform common raw materials such as oil, gas, coal, minerals, air, and water cheaply and efficiently into chemicals that can be used in the manufacture of other things. At a chemical plant, the reactants—or feedstock—are combined under appropriate conditions to produce the desired product.

Curriculum Context

For most curricula, students need to know that reaction rate is the rate of decrease in concentration of reactants or the rate of increase in concentration of products, and that these reciprocal changes form a balanced equation that reflects the conservation of matter.

Yield

A percentage calculated as the amount of product compared to the amount of feedstock used to produce that product.

Increasing reaction rate

It is important to find ways to make reactions occur efficiently, and to increase the reaction rate, which is measured in terms of the change in concentration of a reactant or a product over time. This can sometimes be achieved by increasing the concentration of the reactants, carrying out the reactions at higher temperatures or pressures, or using catalysts that make it easier for the reactants to react with each other at lower temperatures. The aim is to obtain the optimum yield.

However, the optimum yield is not necessarily the maximum yield that can be achieved. When designing a plant, chemical engineers must consider the costs of maintaining the high pressures and temperatures needed to maximize the reaction rate for some products, and the fact that fast exothermic reactions can be very difficult to control. Plant operators and chemical engineers must weigh up safety and energy costs when choosing the reaction conditions.

Batch processing and continuous processing

Chemical engineers must also determine which type of processing to use. In a batch process, raw materials are put into a vessel and allowed to react. When the reaction is complete, the product is removed and new feedstock is added for the next batch. In a continuous process, feedstock is constantly fed into the plant, where it reacts to give a continuous flow of product. Batch processes are useful for slow reactions that produce relatively small amounts of product. Pharmaceutical products and cosmetics are typically manufactured in this way. They are also useful for manufacturing products with which there is an explosion risk, or for fermentation processes in which there is a risk of contamination.

A typical chemical processing plant is a mass of distillation towers, pressurized reaction vessels, and connecting piping.

Continuous processes are an efficient means of high-tonnage production. For example, the important industrial chemicals ammonia and chlorine are manufactured in this way. However, continuous processes require tailor-made plants, and these are expensive to set up.

The Haber Process

The Haber process is a continuous process on an industrial scale in which nitrogen (N_2) is combined with hydrogen (H_2) to make ammonia (NH_3). Nitrogen derived from air is mixed with hydrogen made from natural gas (methane, CH_4). The heated gases are pressurized and passed over a catalyst. The pressure and catalyst lower the activation energy and make it possible to carry out the reaction at lower temperatures. Not all of the hydrogen and nitrogen react during the process—unreacted feedstock is returned to the reaction vessel.

The ammonia must be removed as it is formed, and the reaction must be run at carefully controlled temperatures and pressures of around 752°F (400°C) and 250 atmospheres to ensure that ammonia is formed faster than it decomposes. The process is named after the German chemist Fritz Haber (1868–1934), who won the Nobel Prize for Chemistry in 1918 for his development of the process. Haber also developed ways of producing chlorine and other poisonous gases during World War II. This led to him being known as the "father of chemical warfare."

Waste and pollution

Waste is an inevitable product of all chemical plants. Waste management is therefore an important consideration in all plant design. In the past, operators tended to favor the "dilution solution"—dumping waste into the atmosphere or into rivers, lakes, or oceans, with the hope that it would become sufficiently diluted so as not to be harmful. Now waste is sometimes contained in purpose-built ponds or heaps. However, the waste can contaminate the land or leak into groundwater or rivers. Chemical manufacturers are developing chemical and mechanical waste treatment methods to meet the tougher legal requirements for waste disposal.

Making Useful Chemicals

Common salt (sodium chloride, NaCl) is an essential starting point for the production of many industrial chemicals. Not only is it widely used in the production of caustic soda (sodium hydroxide, NaOH); common salt also forms the basis of another important industrial alkali, sodium carbonate (NaCO$_3$), also known as soda ash or washing soda.

Sodium carbonate

Sodium carbonate has a wide variety of applications. It is used as a source of alkalinity in boiler water to help prevent corrosion, as a water softener, as an ingredient in soaps, detergents, and other cleansing agents, and in photographic developers. Sodium carbonate is also used in steel processing, enameling, textiles, dyes, and food and drink, and in the processing of oils, fats, waxes, and sugars. In addition it is important in the commercial manufacture of glass.

In some parts of the world, sodium carbonate is obtained by mining and purifying trona. This is an evaporite mineral, originally deposited as a result of the evaporation of ancient seas, which contains sodium carbonate, sodium hydrogen carbonate (bicarbonate), and a few impurities. Where trona deposits are not available, synthetic sodium carbonate is manufactured using the Solvay, or ammonia–soda, process.

The Solvay process

The overall reaction used in the Solvay process involves the combination of sodium chloride (NaCl) and calcium carbonate (CaCO$_3$) to produce sodium carbonate (Na$_2$CO$_3$) and calcium chloride (CaCl$_2$). The process includes a number of intermediate steps and requires the input of ammonia, generally manufactured using the Haber process (see page 44), to prevent the favored reverse reaction from taking place.

Evaporite
A kind of sedimentary rock resulting from the evaporation of surface water, leaving behind a mineral deposit.

Sodium carbonate is manufactured using the Solvay process. This technique takes advantage of the overall reaction: $2NaCl + CaCO_3 \rightarrow Na_2CO_3 + CaCl_2$.

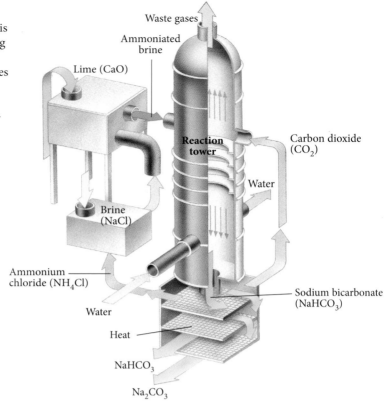

Sodium carbonate made by the Solvay process (above) is one of the main ingredients in glass-making, along with sand (SiO_2), cullet (broken waste glass), limestone ($CaCO_3$), and small amounts of metal oxides. The molten glass is floated on a tank of molten tin to produce perfectly flat sheets.

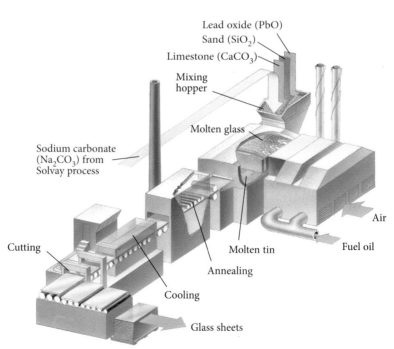

During the Solvay process, a number of useful intermediate products are also produced. The only intermediate product that could be considered waste is calcium chloride ($CaCl_2$), but even this may be used as an energy storage fluid for solar heating systems.

The more widely used intermediate products include ammonium chloride (NH_4Cl), which is often recycled back into the reactor to provide additional ammonia, and sodium hydrogen carbonate ($NaHCO_3$), also known as baking soda or sodium bicarbonate. $NaHCO_3$ is widely used as a raising agent in baking, an antacid agent in indigestion medicines, and as the soda in acid–soda fire extinguishers. It can also be heated to produce a light ash which, when treated with water, produces more crystals of sodium carbonate.

Glass manufacture

Glass is made by heating together sand (SiO_2), limestone ($CaCO_3$), sodium carbonate (Na_2CO_3), cullet (broken waste glass), and small amounts of metal oxides. The metal oxides lower the melting point and alter other characteristics of the glass, such as color. Cobalt oxide produces a blue glass; manganese gives a purple color; copper produces either red or blue-green glass; and chromium gives a green color.

The addition of oxides can also be used to give the glass other characteristics. Lead oxide gives the glass a high refractive index and makes it sparkle because of the greater internal reflection of light, ideal for use in cut glass. Borosilicate glass (Pyrex), a heat-resistant glass that is also resistant to most chemical attack, is made by adding 10–15 percent boron oxide (B_2O_3). Photochromatic sunglasses, which turn darker in the light and lose their color in the dark, are made by incorporating silver chloride ($AgCl$), the active ingredient in photographic film, into the lens glass.

Making Acids and Bases

Some economists claim that the amount of sulfuric acid produced by a nation is a good indicator of its economic health. Whether true or not, there is no doubt that the manufacture of acids and bases for use in a wide range of industrial processes is one of the most important activities of the chemical industry.

Sulfuric acid

Sulfuric acid (H_2SO_4) is probably the leading product of the chemical industry, and most of the sulfur produced worldwide is used for its manufacture. In the United States, for example, almost twice as much sulfuric acid is produced as any other chemical.

Sulfuric acid is one of the strongest acids known, and has a wide range of applications in almost all manufacturing processes. It is commonly used in the manufacture of dyes, paints, paper pulp, explosives, car batteries, and fertilizers. It is also used to make some detergents and in petroleum and metal refining. It is an excellent dehydrating agent, and dissolves many metals to form a wide variety of industrial compounds.

Sulfuric acid is manufactured by the contact process. Here, sulfur is first burned in dry air to form sulfur dioxide (SO_2) gas. The hot SO_2 is reacted with more oxygen at a temperature of around 842°F (450°C) and in the presence of a vanadium oxide (V_2O_5) catalyst to form sulfur trioxide (SO_3). Sulfuric acid can be formed by reacting the SO_3 with water, but this reaction is very violent and forms a mist of sulfuric acid droplets that is difficult to absorb. Instead, SO_3 is dissolved in concentrated (98 percent solution) sulfuric acid, where it reacts less violently. The resulting product is oleum ($H_2S_2O_7$), which is used in some industrial processes. To make sulfuric acid, the oleum is diluted with water to form concentrated sulfuric acid.

Caustic soda

Among the bases, caustic soda (sodium hydroxide, NaOH) is one of the most important. It is widely used in processes including the manufacture of soap, paper, detergents, and other chemicals as well as for the production of rayon and acetate fibers.

Caustic soda (NaOH) is produced in chloralkali plants by the electrolysis of brine—a solution (about 25 percent by mass) of sodium chloride (NaCl). In the process, electricity is passed through the brine in an electrolytic cell. Sodium collects at the cathode, where it reacts with water to form sodium ions and release hydrogen gas and hydroxide ions. As the reaction proceeds, a mixed solution of NaCl and NaOH is formed. This is concentrated in large evaporators, where the NaCl crystallizes out and is removed by filtration. During the process, chlorine gas evolves at the anode, where it is cooled to condense out most of the water and "scrubbed" with sulfuric acid to make a saleable product in its own right. It is widely used for the production of the plastic polyvinyl chloride (PVC).

One important use of sulfuric acid is in car batteries. The electrolyte is sulfuric acid, and the electrodes are made of lead and lead oxide (PbO). As the battery discharges, lead sulfate ($PbSO_4$) builds up on both plates and water builds up in the acid.

Soaps and Detergents

Cleaning products were among the earliest chemicals produced commercially. Soaps were originally manufactured by boiling animal fat and lye, the alkali leached out of wood ash. Today the lye is replaced by the alkali caustic soda (sodium hydroxide, NaOH), and vegetable oils replace the animal fat, but the basic chemistry remains the same.

For many purposes, detergents may be used in place of soap. Hard water contains calcium and magnesium compounds, which form a scum with soap; detergents do not form scum. Scum is not only messy, but also wastes soap, because soap does not lather until it has reacted with all the dissolved substances in the water.

Soaps

Soaps are produced by a chemical reaction called saponification. An ester—a compound formed by the reaction of an acid with an alcohol—reacts with caustic soda to produce soap and the original alcohol. Even now, as in the past, most soaps are made from natural oils and fats. By contrast, detergents are produced from hydrocarbons extracted from petroleum.

Soap is a mixture of the salts of long-chain carboxylic acids—organic acids that have a hydrophilic, or water-soluble, polar carboxyl group ($-COOH$) at one end (the head), and a hydrophobic, or water-insoluble, nonpolar grease-loving group at the other (the tail). In chemical terms, soaps are defined as the sodium salts of long-chain fatty acids, and have the general formula $RCOO^-Na^+$, where R is a long hydrophobic hydrocarbon chain.

Detergents

Like soaps, detergent molecules have a fairly long nonpolar tail and a polar head. But in detergents, also known as synthetic surfactants, the nonpolar tails are produced by a series of chemical reactions on hydrocarbons. By altering the chemical composition, the properties of a detergent can be tailor-made for different cleaning jobs.

Modern laundry detergents include foam stabilizers; water softeners, to counteract the activity of calcium and magnesium ions in hard water; and organic binders, such as sodium carboxymethyl cellulose, to ensure dirt stays in suspension. These work by increasing the negative charge in fabrics, which then repel the negatively charged dirt particles. Some laundry detergents contain "optical brighteners." These substances are molecules that fluoresce—absorb light at one wavelength and emit it at another—to give a blue or ultraviolet light. Optical brighteners overcome

Oil tanker spills at sea can cause great harm to wildlife such as this guillemot, whose feathers are clogged with oil. Detergent can help with the cleaning by breaking the oil into droplets.

any yellow tinge in the fabric, restore the mixture of colors to those that a white fabric would normally reflect, and—in advertising terminology—make white fabrics look "brighter than bright." Biological laundry detergents also contain enzymes—biological catalysts that break down and "digest" substances such as proteins, blood, and sweat.

Action of detergents

When a soap or detergent goes to work on a greasy cloth, its molecules plug their hydrophobic tails into the droplets of grease attached to the fibers. Eventually, the soap molecules surround the droplets to form spherical micelles, which float off the cloth and can be washed away. The detergent also acts as an emulsifier and carries the grease away in solution.

Shampoos

For use as a shampoo, a detergent must be designed to act rather differently. Shampoos must remove oil and dirt while at the same time leaving a thin coating of the natural oil sebum; if too much sebum is washed away, the hair will dry out. Shampoos for greasy hair are designed to remove more of the sebum, whereas for dry hair they are designed to remove less. Shampoo for dry hair often contains fatty material to supplement the natural sebum in the hair.

The acidity of the detergent is also important. Shampoos must be designed to be neutral (with a pH of around 7), because more alkaline compounds, with a higher pH, make the individual strands of hair break easily, and ruffle the outer surface of the hair, which can make it look dull and coarse.

Curriculum Context

For most curricula, students should know that a pH scale indicates with numbers the concentration of hydrogen ions in a solution, and characterizes a solution as acidic (lower than 7), alkaline (higher than 7), or neutral (near 7).

Organic Compounds

Millions of years ago, carbon compounds in the atmosphere formed an insulating blanket around the Earth, which trapped the Sun's heat. This gradually made the Earth warm enough for life to evolve. Carbon remains central to life, although it makes up less than 1 percent of the Earth. The molecules that make up all living things are based on carbon compounds.

Carbon circulates through plants, animals, the soil, and the atmosphere in a process known as the carbon cycle. Carbon dioxide is released into the atmosphere when biomass fuels such as wood, or fossil fuels such as oil, gas, and coal, are burned to release energy. Carbon-based fuels account for 75 percent of the energy used on the planet today.

Curriculum Context

For many curricula, students should know about the global carbon cycle: the different physical and chemical forms of carbon in the atmosphere, oceans, biomass, and in fossil fuels, and the movement of carbon among these reservoirs.

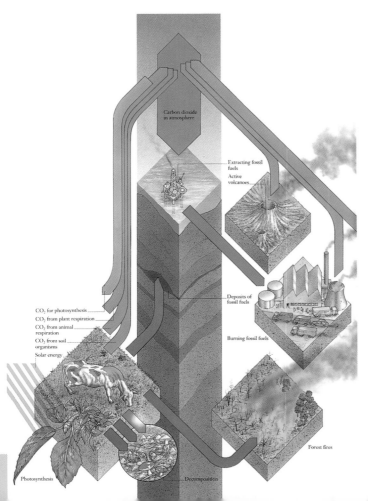

Carbon dioxide in atmosphere

Extracting fossil fuels

Active volcanoes

Deposits of fossil fuels

Burning fossil fuels

CO₂ for photosynthesis
CO₂ from plant respiration
CO₂ from animal respiration
CO₂ from soil organisms
Solar energy

Forest fires

Photosynthesis

Decomposition

In the carbon cycle, carbon moves between the air, the oceans, the ground, and living things. Plants take up carbon dioxide from the air, while animals breathe it out. Large amounts of carbon are locked up in fossil fuel deposits; burning fossil fuels releases this as carbon dioxide. Carbon dioxide dissolves in the oceans, while volcanoes release clouds of carbon dioxide into the atmosphere.

Organic chemistry

Carbon is versatile because each carbon atom forms four covalent bonds. Organic molecules (so called because chemists once thought that these compounds could only be found in living organisms) are made up of carbon atoms bonded together by single, double, or triple covalent bonds. The range of compounds formed by these bonded carbon atoms is the basis of organic chemistry. The different combinations of carbon atoms are almost endless, especially because organic compounds can form isomers—molecules that have the same chemical formula as each other, but have a different structure. Different isomers have different physical properties, and sometimes they can have different chemical properties as well.

Homologous series

To make sense of all this variation, organic chemists group organic molecules containing carbon atoms bonded in the same way into families known as homologous series. All members of a given series have the same general molecular formula and similar chemical properties. However, physical properties, such as melting point, boiling point, and density, gradually change as the number of carbon atoms increases.

Aliphatic

A term for carbon compounds that do not contain aromatic (benzene-like) rings.

The simplest group of carbon compounds is the aliphatic hydrocarbons, which contain only hydrogen and carbon atoms arranged in straight or branched chains. This group include the alkanes, alkenes, and alkynes. But behind their simple formulas lies a great deal of variety.

Alkanes

The alkanes (formerly called paraffins) are saturated hydrocarbons. This means that the hydrogen and carbon atoms are joined only by single bonds. The alkane series has the general formula C_nH_{n+2}, where n represents the number of carbon atoms. It begins with methane (CH_4). Each subsequent compound in the series has one more carbon atom and two more hydrogen atoms than the one before. The next few members, all gases, are ethane (C_2H_6), propane (C_3H_8), and butane (C_4H_{10}). From pentane (C_5H_{12}) onward, the alkanes are liquids. The highest members of the series take the form of waxy solids.

Alkanes are important fuels. They burn cleanly and give off a great deal of energy. Natural gas is composed mainly of the alkane methane (CH_4), though it may also contain heavier alkanes such as ethane (C_2H_6) and propane (C_3H_8). Larger alkanes, such as octane (C_8H_{18}), give off more energy per molecule than smaller alkanes, because they contain more bonds to be broken.

Alkanes are called saturated molecules because it is impossible to add other atoms to them. Saturated molecules are not very reactive, but alkanes can participate in substitution reactions, in which other atoms change places with one or more of the alkane's hydrogen atoms.

Alkenes

Alkenes (formerly called olefins) are hydrocarbons that have a double bond between two of their carbon atoms. They have the general formula C_nH_{2n}. Alkenes are unsaturated, and are thus more reactive than the alkanes. They typically participate in addition reactions, during which the double bond between the carbon atoms is broken and other atoms are added. Alkenes can be hydrated to form carbohydrates, also known as alcohols. In this reaction, water reacts with an alkene in the presence of the catalyst sulfuric acid, to form a single-bonded carbon molecule that includes an –OH group.

The smallest alkene molecule, ethene (ethylene, C_2H_4), is probably one of the best known. It is produced

Oxy-acetylene welding torches use the reaction between oxygen and acetylene to produce a very hot flame (up to 6,300°F, 3,500°C).

industrially during the refining of crude oil, and forms the basis of many familiar plastics, such as polythene (polyethene), used for carrier bags, and polystyrene, which is often used as an insulating material. Ethene is also the basis for dry-cleaning fluid (tetrachloroethene, CCl_4, also called perchloroethylene or perc) and antifreeze (ethylene glycol, now more correctly called ethane-1,2-diol, CH_2OHCH_2OH).

Alkynes

The most reactive hydrocarbons are the alkynes (formerly called acetylenes), general formula C_nH_{2n-2}. Alkynes contain a relatively unstable carbon–carbon triple bond, which gives off lots of energy when broken. The smallest molecule in the series, ethyne (acetylene, C_2H_2), is used in oxy-acetylene torches for welding, because it burns with an intense flame that is hot enough to melt most substances, including metals. An oxy-acetylene torch will even work underwater, although electric arc welders are more often used.

Carbon–Hydrogen Compounds

Compounds that contain hydrogen and carbon provide nearly three-quarters of the energy needs of the planet, and are the most popular form of energy in use today. The energy contained in hydrocarbons was originally trapped from the Sun by ancient plants during photosynthesis that took place millions of years ago. It was converted to chemical energy by plants, and is now preserved in the chemical bonds that hold together the molecules in fossilized hydrocarbon fuels such as oil, gas, and coal.

Fossil fuel formation

Fossil fuels are formed as the result of millions of years of heat and pressure on the remains of dead plants and animals. After they died, the plants and animals were buried by silt and mud, which kept out oxygen and prevented decay. Instead, the organic matter was broken down by anaerobic bacteria, which thrive in the absence of oxygen. The matter gradually became buried by sediments.

As the deposits were buried deeper, the pressure increased, and the temperature rose. Over millions of years, the material was slowly cooked and converted into long, complex chains of hydrogen and carbon.

The type of hydrocarbon that is formed during the long, slow "cooking" process depends partly on the chemistry of the original organic material, and partly on the conditions of temperature and pressure under which it was buried. Coal is generally formed as a result of the burial of plants in primeval swamps, and is made up of a mixture of complex hydrocarbons with a high content of carbon. Both oil and gas are more typically generated by the decay and burial of tiny sea animals such as plankton, although gas can also be generated during the burial of coal swamps. Oil contains less carbon and more hydrogen than coal.

Curriculum Context

Many curricula expect students to know that chemical reactions may release or consume energy. Some reactions, such as the burning of fossil fuels, release large amounts of energy by losing heat and by emitting light.

Plankton

Marine organisms that are either microscopic or very small, which drift or weakly swim with the ocean currents rather than against them.

Crude oil, pumped from the pore spaces between grains in reservoir rocks buried deep underground, is a mixture of many different kinds of hydrocarbon molecules. Most crude oil is extracted from the ground to make fuel, but around 10 percent is used as a feedstock, or raw material, in the chemical industry. Before it can be used, the various hydrocarbon molecules are separated by refining.

Oil refining

At a refinery, crude oil is separated into different fractions—groups of hydrocarbons that have different boiling points (a function of the number of carbon atoms they contain). The separation takes place in a fractional distillation column, or fractionating tower.

During the fractionation process, crude oil heated to around 644°F (350°C) is introduced into the base of the column. As it boils, oil vapor rises up the column, and cools. Different fractions condense at different heights in the column, where they can be separated.

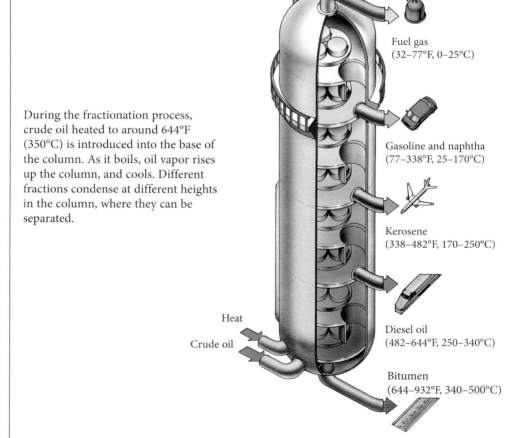

Fuel gas
(32–77°F, 0–25°C)

Gasoline and naphtha
(77–338°F, 25–170°C)

Kerosene
(338–482°F, 170–250°C)

Diesel oil
(482–644°F, 250–340°C)

Bitumen
(644–932°F, 340–500°C)

Heat

Crude oil

During the refining operation, crude oil heated to a temperature of around 660°F (350°C) is introduced at the base of the tower. As it boils, the oil vapor passes up the column; as it rises, it cools.

The different fractions cool and condense at different temperatures, and therefore at different heights up the column. Light hydrocarbons condense first, near the top of the column. They include petroleum gas or fuel gas (between 1 and 4 carbon atoms), which condenses at around 55°F (13°C) and is used as bottled gas; gasoline (between 5 and 10 carbon atoms), which condenses at around 158°F (70°C); and naphtha, used in chemical manufacture, which condenses at around 284°F (140°C). The middle fractions (338–644°F, 170–340°C) include kerosene, used in jet fuel; paraffin; diesel oil; and fuel oil, used for heating. Heavy fractions, such as lubricating oil and bitumen (asphalt), condense above 644°F (350°C).

Zeolites

Complex minerals called zeolites are sometimes used in the refining process to help separate out specific hydrocarbon molecules. Zeolites are ideal for this job because their crystal structure includes pores of specific sizes into which cations (positively charged ions) can fit. Zeolites can be easily modified by replacing some of the atoms in their crystal structure with other elements. This makes it possible for chemists to "design" zeolites that work as very effective molecular sieves for precise purposes, separating out specific types of molecules by size and shape. Alternatively, zeolites can be used as catalysts with molecules of specific sizes.

Although they occur naturally in volcanic rocks, for refinery use zeolites are generally made in the laboratory, where it is possible to produce them with precise pore sizes and shapes.

Carbon, Hydrogen, and Oxygen

A glass of wine, a potato, and the sugar in coffee all contain compounds of carbon, hydrogen, and oxygen. In wine, the compound is alcohol; in potatoes, it is the carbohydrate starch; and the sugar added to coffee is sucrose. Carbohydrates, like hydrocarbons, can be very large molecules. However, unlike hydrocarbons, they also contain oxygen, usually in the ratio of two atoms of hydrogen to one of oxygen.

Curriculum Context

For most curricula, students are expected to know how to identify the functional groups that form the basis of alcohols, ketones, ethers, amines, esters, aldehydes, and organic acids.

Alcohols

Alcohols contain the hydroxyl (−OH) functional group. Ethanol (ethyl alcohol, C_2H_5OH), the alcohol in beverages, is used in industry as a solvent for paints, dyes, and perfumes; in medicine as an antiseptic and solvent for many drugs; and in some countries as a fuel, because it produces a lot of heat and does not give off polluting sulfur and nitrous oxides.

Ethanol itself is the product of a reaction involving sugar, another carbohydrate. All sugars contain the basic units $C_6H_{12}O_6$, but differ from each other in the arrangement of atoms in their molecules. The various sugars have different properties. For thousands of years, ethanol has been made by fermenting sugar with yeast. During fermentation, enzymes in the yeast act as catalysts to break down the sugar into ethanol and carbon dioxide (CO_2).

Ethanol for industrial use is also made by combining a hydrocarbon, the alkene ethene (C_2H_4), with steam (H_2O) to cause an addition reaction in which an −OH functional group is added.

Aldehydes

Aldehydes can be made by oxidizing an alcohol (removing hydrogen atoms from it). In aldehydes, the functional group is a carbonyl group, −C=O, in which a carbon atom is doubly bonded to an oxygen atom. The carbonyl group is generally linked to two hydrogen atoms or to one hydrogen atom and a hydrocarbon radical.

Aldehydes are easily oxidized and are often used as reducing agents. Formaldehyde (methanal, HCHO), one of the most familiar aldehydes, is a preservative and an important component in plastics. Urea-formaldehyde and melamine-formaldehyde resins are used, for example, in paints, lacquers, and adhesives.

Esters

Alcohol reacts with water and any of the organic acids that contain a carboxyl group (–COOH) to form esters—compounds that give flowers their sweet scent and are the basis of many of the "natural" fruit flavors used in food processing. Esters are also important solvents, which are widely used in the cosmetic and pharmaceutical industries. Fats are esters with higher molecular weight than the others, and function as food reserves in some plants and animals.

Radical

In organic chemistry, radicals are groups of atoms that attach themselves to different compounds as if they were one element, and remain unchanged internally during chemical reactions.

Sugar cane being harvested. Sugar cane is the main source of sucrose (table sugar). Sucrose is a combination of two other common sugars: glucose and fructose. These two sugars are isomers: they have the same empirical formula ($C_6H_{12}O_6$) but different structures.

Aromatic Compounds

In the aliphatic carbon-based molecules, each carbon atom exhibits its ability to form four covalent bonds with other atoms. This makes it possible for the aliphatic compounds to form straight or branched chains. But in aromatic compounds, carbon exhibits the ability to form strong bonds with itself. As a result, carbon atoms can form rings as well as straight and branched chains. Because some natural oils that contain carbon rings smell sweet, such carbon-ring compounds were named aromatic organic compounds.

Unsaturated compound

An organic compound containing double or triple bonds, which make it more reactive than a saturated compound (one containing only single bonds).

Benzene

Benzene (C_6H_6), one of the simplest and most important aromatics, has a pungent and unpleasant smell, and there is evidence that it can cause cancer, particularly in young children. Benzene forms the basis of many compounds, but chemists have only recently understood the nature of the bonding in this relatively common molecule. It consists of six carbon atoms joined in a hexagonal ring, with a hydrogen atom bonded to each carbon. The electrons involved in part of the carbon–carbon bonding are said to be delocalized, and are not associated with any particular carbon atom. As a result, the chemical behavior of benzene can be surprising. For example, although it is highly unsaturated, benzene is much less reactive than expected, and has its own characteristic properties. Because of the nature of the bonding, benzene tends to undergo reactions that preserve the stable ring.

Benzene derivatives

Benzene rings form the basis of a wide range of aromatic compounds, because other atoms or groups of atoms can be substituted into the ring to replace one or more of the hydrogens. Many useful benzene derivatives have been developed, including chemicals used in plastics and dyes (phenylamine or aniline, benzene with an $-NH_2$ group substituted in the ring), rubbers, resins, perfumes (nitrobenzene, benzene with an $-NO_2$ group substituted), preservatives, and flavoring agents (benzaldehyde, benzene with a $-CHO$ group substituted). Substituting a hydroxyl ($-OH$) group into benzene produces phenol, a disinfectant formerly called carbolic acid.

Steroids

Steroids—widely known as muscle-building drugs used illegally by some athletes—are organic compounds whose central molecule contains four carbon rings (a sterol), sometimes with side-chains attached. Steroids include human sex hormones and bile salts; plant alkaloids such as caffeine and nicotine; and the insect hormone ecdysone, which controls molting. All steroid hormones are based on cholesterol.

There is little chemical difference between the male sex hormone testosterone and the female hormone progesterone; the latter contains one extra oxygen atom.

Anabolic steroids are hormones that have been used in the past by many athletes, especially those in power sports such as weightlifting. They can increase muscle bulk and power, in combination with exercise. However, the drugs give an unfair advantage, and they have adverse side effects. The use of such drugs is now banned by nearly all sporting bodies.

The carbon–carbon bonds in benzene are unique—they are neither double nor single bonds. The benzene ring is a flat hexagon with six C–C bonds all of the same length. Some of the electrons involved in the bonding are said to be delocalized. They are not associated with any particular carbon atom, but are shared by all six carbon atoms in the ring. The delocalized electrons make two doughnut-shaped "clouds" above and below the plane of the benzene ring. A benzene ring is shown here viewed from three different perspectives. The cloud of delocalized electrons is clearly visible.

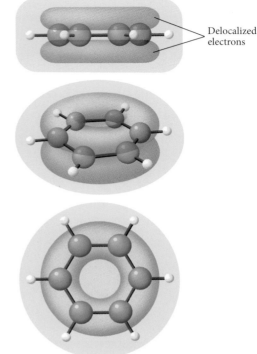

Delocalized electrons

● Carbon atom

○ Hydrogen atom

Curriculum Context

Most curricula expect students to know that benzene, C_6H_6, is a flat, hexagonally shaped molecule of six carbon atoms bonded to each other, and that many compounds can be built by substitutions on benzene rings.

Aromatic polymers

Benzene is also an important molecule in plastics and polymers. Benzene added to the alkene ethene (C_2H_4) forms the basis of phenylethene (styrene), the building block of the polymer polystyrene. This important synthetic polymer is made up of benzene rings arranged along the length of a chain of carbon atoms.

Polystyrene can be used to make molded objects and electrical insulators. Because it is clear and can be colored easily, it is often used for optical components. Benzene rings can also join together to give fused ring systems which, like benzene itself, can participate in addition and substitution reactions to form a wide range of other compounds. In these systems the delocalization of the electrons extends over all the rings. Compounds of this type include naphthalene, which consists of two benzene rings fused together. Naphthalene is used in plasticizers, alkyd resins, polyesters, insecticides, and mothballs.

Heterocyclic Compounds

The six carbon atoms in a molecule of benzene, described on the previous pages, are arranged in the form of a ring. Benzene is an example of a cyclic compound. Other cyclic compounds that, like benzene, contain only carbon and hydrogen include cyclobutane, C_4H_8, and cyclohexane, C_6H_{12}. But the rings of cyclic compounds can contain atoms other than carbon—so-called hetero (meaning "different") atoms such as oxygen, nitrogen, and sulfur.

Cyclic compounds containing atoms other than carbon are called heterocyclic compounds, and there can be more than one hetero atom in a single ring. Such compounds commonly occur in nature as sugars, alkaloids, and vitamins, and as part of the gene-building nucleic acids such as DNA. Synthetic heterocyclic compounds have many uses, including as drugs, dyes, pesticides, and (as polymers) plastics.

Pyran and furan rings

One of the simplest heterocyclic compounds is pyran, whose molecule is a six-membered ring with five carbon atoms and one oxygen atom. It forms part of the structure of many sugars (saccharides), such as glucose and its isomer fructose. Furan has a five-membered ring (four carbons and one oxygen) and it, too, forms part of a sugar, the fairly unstable furanose. Adding an aldehyde group (–CHO) to furan produces furfural, which occurs in many essential oils. It is made commercially by heating corn cobs or oat husks with steam under pressure, and combined with phenol (C_6H_5OH) to make artificial resins.

Pyridines and pyrroles

By far the most numerous heterocyclic compounds have nitrogen as their hetero atoms. A six-membered ring with five carbon atoms and a single nitrogen atom is the evil-smelling, poisonous compound

Curriculum Context

For many curricula, students should know that carbon atoms can bond to one another in chains, rings, and branching networks to form a variety of structures, including synthetic polymers, oils, and the large molecules essential to life.

A heterocyclic compound can have from 3 to more than 20 atoms in the ring, although 5- and 6-atom rings are by far the most common. Nitrogen and oxygen are the most common hetero atoms, although sulfur and phosphorus also occur in some natural compounds.

pyridine, which occurs naturally as part of vitamin B6 (pyridoxine) and the alkaloids morphine, nicotine, and quinine. It was originally made by strongly heating bones—the *pyr-* part of the name comes from *pur*, the Greek word for fire—but is today synthesized commercially from ethyne (acetylene) and ammonia. It is used as a solvent in the plastics industry and as a starting material for making drugs and nicotinic acid (also called niacin, one of the B vitamins). Other derivatives include vinyl-pyridine, which is used to make synthetic rubber, and the weedkiller paraquat.

A pyrrole is a five-membered ring compound that has four carbon atoms and a single nitrogen atom. Like benzene, pyrroles are aromatic compounds, used mainly to make drugs and dyes. Pyrroles also occur widely in nature in various highly colored substances, such as green chlorophyll and heme, which is part of hemoglobin. Hemoglobin is the pigment that gives the red color to blood; its function is to latch onto oxygen

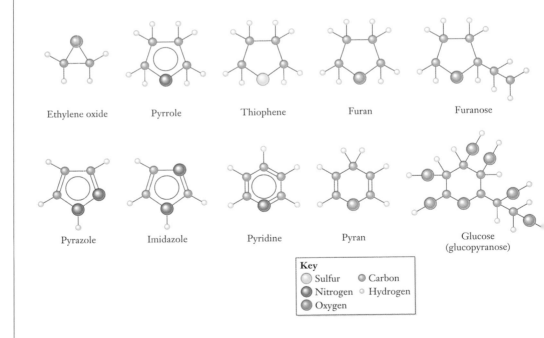

Ethylene oxide   Pyrrole   Thiophene   Furan   Furanose

Pyrazole   Imidazole   Pyridine   Pyran   Glucose (glucopyranose)

Key
- Sulfur
- Nitrogen
- Oxygen
- Carbon
- Hydrogen

in the lungs and carry it to the tissues. The heme molecule consists of four pyrrole derivatives surrounding an iron atom.

Imidazole and pyrazole

Imidazole and pyrazole have five-membered rings that include three carbon atoms and two nitrogen atoms. In pyrazole, the nitrogens are next door to each other; in imidazole, they are next door but one. Pyrazole is an aromatic compound and forms part of the important molecules adenine and guanine, which are bases in the DNA molecule. Drugs derived from pyrazole include the fever-reducing antipyrine and the anti-inflammatory phenylbutazone. Another derivative is the yellow dye tartrazine, which is commonly employed to color foodstuffs and is associated with hyperactivity in some children.

Compounds with two nitrogen atoms in a six-membered ring include cytosine, thymine, and uracil, the other bases in molecules of DNA or RNA.

Smaller heterocyclic rings

Heterocyclic rings containing fewer than five atoms are less stable because the bonds in the rings are strained through small angles. Examples include penicillins and some other antibiotics, which have nitrogen-containing four-membered rings, and ethylene oxide (used to make epoxy resins and ethylene glycol for antifreeze), which has a three-membered ring with two carbon atoms and one oxygen atoms.

Stable rings can also be made with seven or more atoms, such as the porphyrins that make up the skeletons of hemoglobin and chlorophyll molecules. There are also a few heterocyclic compounds with phosphorus as their hetero atom, and some of these are proving useful as anticancer drugs.

Making Hydrocarbons

Adding or subtracting hydrogen atoms can make a big difference to the preparation of edible oils and fats. At room temperature, oils are liquids, whereas fats are solids. The physical difference between an edible oil, such as olive oil or sunflower oil, and a solid fat, like margarine, is largely a difference in the number of hydrogen atoms they contain.

Oils and fats

Edible oils and fats have a similar chemical structure. Both are made up of long chains of carbon atoms with hydrogen atoms attached. Oils, are more unsaturated than fats—they have a higher proportion of double bonds and fewer hydrogen atoms. The double C=C bonds are less stable than single bonds and help give oils a lower melting point. This is why oils are liquids at room temperature. Fats, on the other hand, are said to be saturated: all their carbon atoms are involved in single bonds. As a result, they have a higher melting point, and are solids at room temperature.

Hydrogenation

Adding hydrogen to oils to change them to fats is called hydrogenation. The oil is first heated to 302°F (150°C), and a powdered nickel catalyst is added. When hydrogen is bubbled through the oil, it causes the double C=C bonds to break. The carbon atoms begin to form new single bonds with the hydrogen. The more hydrogen that is used, the more double bonds are broken. To produce a hard fat, hydrogen is added until the oil is fully saturated. To produce a softer fat, with a lower melting point, less hydrogen is added.

Margarine

Margarine is an emulsion that contains droplets of water, skim milk, and brine suspended in oil and fat. An emulsifier is used to make the oil and water mix.

Soft margarines are "high in polyunsaturates"— they are made up of fats and oils that contain many double bonds. Such fats and oils are easily spread, and many doctors believe that they are healthier than saturated fats, which can increase the risk of heart disease. However, in many margarines the polyunsaturates are partially hydrogenated to make them more solid. This leads to the production of particular types of fatty acids called trans fatty acids. Research has shown that these carry an increased risk of heart disease.

Hydrogenating coal

Edible oils are not the only substances that can be hydrogenated. Coal can be hydrogenated by a process called liquefaction to produce a liquid fuel. This can then be refined to produce gasoline, diesel fuel, jet fuel, fuel oils, and petrochemicals. In a liquefaction process called the Bergius process, pulverized coal is suspended in a liquid mixture of hydrocarbons. The slurry is then hydrogenated by being heated and exposed to gaseous hydrogen under pressure.

One of the main uses of sunflowers is to produce vegetable oil and margarine. To make vegetable oil the sunflower oil is partially hydrogenated to stabilize it and produce a more solid consistency.

Natural Polymers

All living things contain polymers: proteins, carbohydrates, wood, and natural rubber are all polymers. What nature has invented, chemists have learned to copy and manipulate successfully. It is now possible to make a vast range of synthetic polymers.

Macromolecule

A giant molecule formed by joining together multiple copies of one or more smaller molecules in single or branched chains.

What are polymers?

Polymers are large organic macromolecules that usually contain carbon and hydrogen, often together with oxygen and nitrogen. They are made up of smaller repeating units known as monomers. Some polymers, called homopolymers, contain just one monomer; but others, known as copolymers, are made up of two or more types of monomers. During polymerization, the monomers join up to make long chains. Although polymers can contain as few as five repeating units, most are made up of several thousand.

The nature of the groups of atoms that make up a polymer determines the characteristics of the polymer. The molecules in the chain can form bonds with each other, both along their length and between chains. These intermolecular forces give different polymers their individual characteristics.

Curriculum Context

For many curricula, students should know that large molecules (polymers), such as proteins, nucleic acids, and starch, are formed by repetitive combinations of simple subunits.

Rubber

Natural polymers are everywhere—in fact, many of them grow on trees. The sap obtained from rubber trees provided the raw material for one of the earliest polymer industries: rubber production. Natural rubber, or latex, known to chemists as polyisoprene, is a polymer made up of 1,000–5,000 monomers of the unsaturated hydrocarbon isoprene (C_5H_8), which is obtained from the sap of the rubber tree. Isoprene contains two double bonds separated by a single bond. When it polymerizes, bonds are broken and rearranged to allow the monomers to link up in a long, coiled chain. This chain gives rubber its physical properties.

Rubber is elastic because stretching tends to straighten out the entangled chains, but when the stretching force is released, the intermolecular forces pull the chains back together. The tangled chains are also what gives rubber its ability to hold together when stretched, rather than breaking or crumbling. The fact that rubber is made up of a dense tangle of hydrophobic hydrocarbon chains also accounts for its waterproof properties.

Natural rubber softens on heating and hardens on cooling without changing its chemical properties. It is used in cements and adhesives, and as tape for wrapping cables and insulating electrical equipment. However, because it has a relatively low melting point, natural rubber softens in warm weather.

Vulcanization

The process of vulcanization is used to raise rubber's low melting point, and to make it hard enough for use in tires and other products. During vulcanization, the long chains of polyisoprene units are linked together by sulfur bonds. This cross-linking makes the rubber more thermally stable, but changes it into a material that cannot be altered once molded or formed without destroying its properties. A further drawback is that vulcanized rubber has a relatively short lifetime, because the sulfur bridges react readily with the oxygen in air. As a result, natural rubber is largely

Natural Composites

Chemists can combine a polymer with another material to produce a composite with special properties, often for engineering applications. Fiberglass is a composite in which thin glass fibers are bound together in an unsaturated polyester resin. This process occurs in nature, too. One of the most abundant natural polymer composites is a cellulose fiber-reinforced phenylic resin composite—best known under its common name, wood.

Cotton, shown here being harvested, comprises fibers of cellulose, the structural ingredient in most plant cells. The orientation of the glucose monomers in the cellulose polymer alternates, resulting in strong fibers.

being replaced by synthetic rubber substitutes, such as nitrile and chloroprene rubbers, produced from petroleum. These synthetic versions have higher melting points and a longer lifetime, and are far less affected by organic solvents.

Cellulose and starch

Cellulose and starch are other important natural polymers that grow on trees. Both are based on the monomer glucose, a simple sugar formed by plants during photosynthesis (see pages 101–103). Starch is used by both plants and animals as an energy store. When energy is needed, the starch can be easily broken down into glucose molecules, which are then oxidized through respiration (see page 86) to release carbon dioxide, water, and energy.

Cellulose is the polymer that makes up the main structural material of plants. It is one of the most abundant organic substances on Earth, and cannot be readily broken down; herbivorous animals that depend on eating cellulose often have special bacteria living in the gut to assist with digestion.

Synthetic Polymers

Imitating nature was the goal of the first polymer chemists, and polymer science evolved as they found ways of synthesizing materials with properties similar to those already available in the natural world. Now, polymer chemists use their knowledge to design molecules to order.

Early synthetics

Initially, chemists concentrated on trying to develop polymers that were less expensive or more readily available substances than the equivalent natural materials; for example, synthetic wood and rubber for use in construction, synthetic cotton and silk to make into clothing and fabrics, and synthetic resins for use in paints and varnishes.

Some of the earliest commercial polymers were based on naturally occurring polymers, such as cellulose. Cellulose is an important structural material in plant cells, and is the major component of wood and cotton. It also forms the basis of one of the first synthetic fibers to be developed—artificial silk, or rayon.

Rayon

The protein fibers that make up natural silk are triangular in cross-section. This gives silk its shiny appearance. Rayon is made from carbohydrate fibers, rather than protein. The fibers are made by treating cellulose, from wood pulp or cotton, with an acid.

In the first form of rayon, the cellulose, mostly derived from purified cotton fibers, was reacted with nitric acid to form cellulose nitrate ("nitrocellulose"), which could be formed into fibers. However, because molecules containing nitro groups are dangerously flammable and even explosive, the cellulose nitrate form of rayon was not ideal for use in clothing.

Today's rayons are much safer. They are produced by reacting cellulose with acetic acid to produce cellulose acetate. This is extruded through spinnerets to form fibers, which can be spun into a yarn and woven to produce the textile rayon acetate.

Synthetic rubber

Synthetic rubbers were developed to find ways of taking advantage of some of the useful properties of natural latex, such as its elasticity and waterproof nature, while at the same time overcoming some of its drawbacks, such as low melting point and relative instability in air. In making synthetic rubber, chemists aimed to replace the isoprene monomers with other hydrocarbons, derived from crude oil.

One common use of neoprene and other synthetic rubbers is for wetsuits and other watersports equipment.

Synthetic rubbers can be made using either emulsion or solution polymerization. In the process of emulsion polymerization, the reaction is carried out in water in the presence of a catalyst, and an emulsion of rubber is formed. In solution polymerization, the reaction takes place in an organic solvent.

Today, roughly 60 percent of rubber is produced synthetically. By choosing monomers carefully, it is possible to make synthetic rubbers with specific properties to suit different applications, and with improved properties of toughness and durability. One of the major rubbers produced today is a copolymer of styrene (C_8H_8) and butadiene (C_4H_6), which is widely used for vehicle tires. Neoprene, an oil-resistant rubber that is not affected by ozone, is made by the polymerization of chloroprene (C_4H_5Cl).

Organic solvent
A solvent that dissolves organic compounds such as hydrocarbons, which are not soluble in water. Common organic solvents include ethyl alcohol (CH_3CH_2OH) and acetone (CH_3COCH_3).

Plastics

Hydrocarbons are also key raw materials in the production of plastics. Nearly 4 percent of crude oil production is used as a raw material for plastics. Crude oil includes a variety of hydrocarbon molecules, which contain varying numbers of carbon and hydrogen atoms. The naphtha fraction (8 to 12 carbon atoms) is the most important for plastics production because it can be "cracked," or broken down into smaller molecules, by passing its vapor through tubes heated to about 1,500°F (800°C) and mixing it with steam.

One of the products of the cracking of naphtha is the alkene ethene (ethylene, C_2H_4)—the single most important substance for producing plastics. The most common of all plastics is polyvinyl chloride (PVC). It is used to insulate electric cables, for audio disks, for waterproof clothing, and for the interior trim of cars. When one of the hydrogens in ethene is replaced by chlorine, the result is chloroethene (vinyl chloride), the monomer at the heart of PVC.

Types of Plastics

Plastics have a wide range of physical properties. Some, like Bakelite, are hard and will not melt. Others, such as polythene, can be made into thin, flexible films. One of the advantages of plastics is that they can be synthesized to have different properties.

Dipole

A weak positive–negative polarity in a covalent molecule.

Hydrogen bond

A weak bond formed between a polarized hydrogen atom and an electronegative atom (one that attracts electrons) such as oxygen.

Curriculum Context

For many curricula, students should know that hydrogen bonding is essential to life and gives water many of its unusual properties. In water, hydrogen bonding occurs between the hydrogen on one water molecule and the oxygen on a neighboring water molecule.

Thermoplastics

The physical properties of plastics are closely related to the molecular structure of the polymer chains and the nature of the forces that link the chains together. Polythene, polystyrene (styrofoam), polyvinyl chloride (PVC), and nylon, which melt on heating, are all thermoplastics. They are made up of long, thin, covalently bonded monomers that form tangled chains. Relatively weak electrostatic forces, including induced dipole forces (see pages 16–17), dipole–dipole forces, and hydrogen bonding, hold the chains together. These forces can easily be destroyed by heat: the plastics soften on warming as the chains begin to move over each other more easily. This is why thermoplastic polymers stretch and flex easily, melt at low temperatures, and melt without decomposing.

Thermosetting plastics

By contrast, thermosetting polymers, such as Bakelite and other methanal (formaldehyde) resins, including urea–formaldehyde and melamine, are made up of cross-linked chains. Strong covalent bonds both within and between the chains form a random three-dimensional network with rigid bonds, which inhibit the chains from moving in relation to one another when they are heated, stretched, or compressed. The covalent bonds between the chains develop as the thermosetting polymers are cured (usually by heating) after they are molded or shaped. Once the bonds have formed between the polymer chains, the plastics become rigid and hard. Their shape cannot be changed, and they burn or char before they melt.

Monomers and Polymers

Oil, natural gas, limestone, salt, and fluorspar are major raw materials in the production of monomers (the simple building blocks of plastics and polymers). The physical properties of polymers can be controlled by changing the types or arrangement of monomers in the chain.

The familiar plastics polythene (polyethylene) and nylon are both straight-chain polymers.

Polythene is made entirely from the monomer ethene (C_2H_4), and contains only carbon and hydrogen. Nylon is a more complex polymer. It is made by combining two different six-carbon monomers, which include nitrogen and oxygen atoms. The linkage that joins the nylon monomers together is called an amine bond. It is the same link that joins amino acids together in proteins.

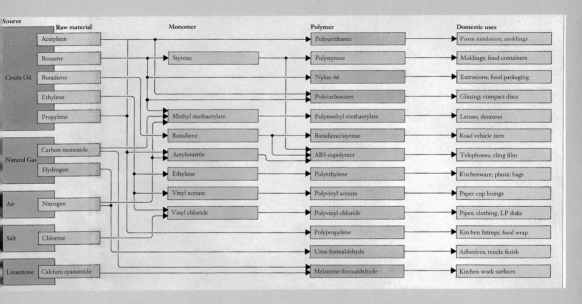

Source	Raw material	Monomer	Polymer	Domestic uses
	Acetylene		Polyurethanes	Foam insulation; moldings
	Benzene	Styrene	Polystyrene	Moldings; food containers
Crude Oil	Butadiene		Nylon 66	Extrusions; food packaging
	Ethylene		Polycarbonates	Glazing; compact discs
	Propylene	Methyl methacrylate	Polymethyl methacrylate	Lenses; dentures
		Butadiene	Butadiene/styrene	Road vehicle tires
	Carbon monoxide	Acrylonitrile	ABS copolymer	Telephones; cling film
Natural Gas	Hydrogen	Ethylene	Polyethylene	Kitchenware; plastic bags
		Vinyl acetate	Polyvinyl acetate	Paper cup linings
Air	Nitrogen	Vinyl chloride	Polyvinyl chloride	Pipes; clothing; LP disks
			Polypropylene	Kitchen fittings; food wrap
Salt	Chlorine		Urea-formaldehyde	Adhesives; textile finish
Limestone	Calcium cyanamide		Melamine-formaldehyde	Kitchen work surfaces

Chain length and branching

The length of a chain and the amount of branching in it also affect the physical properties of a polymer. Increasing the length of the polymer chain tends to produce stronger materials, because longer chains tangle more easily, and thus have more points of contact with neighboring chains. This leads to a greater number of attractive forces between molecules that hold the chains together. The stronger bonds between molecules create a stronger material.

Straight chains can pack together more closely to form high-density polymers that are strong but not very flexible, and that soften at relatively high temperatures. Polymers made of highly branched chains that cannot pack together very closely tend to be less dense, and may be glassy and transparent.

Types of bonding

The nature of the bonding within the chain is another important variable. Polymers normally act as electrical insulators, but in 1976 conducting polymers were developed. These have alternating single and double carbon–carbon bonds in their polymer chains and become electrically conducting when "doped," or treated with chemicals that either donate or remove electrons to leave them partly reduced or oxidized.

Doping
Intentionally introducing small amounts of impurities into a very pure material in order to change its physical properties.

Conducting polymers are already used by two Japanese companies to make small button batteries for cameras and hearing aids. Now research chemists are working to develop polymer blends, or mixtures of conducting and nonconducting polymers. These will result in materials with electrical properties that can be used like normal plastics to produce a wide range of products. Plastics that shield against electromagnetic radiation, plastic electrodes, conducting paints, inks, fibers, and flooring materials are just some of the possible applications.

Shaping Plastics

Once polymers are synthesized, they can be processed in different ways to provide a wide variety of shapes and structures for many uses. For example, nylon can be molded to make syringes or spectacle frames, or drawn into fibers to make stockings.

Drawing and extrusion

Fibers can be made by cold drawing, in which a liquid polymer is stretched into a long, thin filament. Cold drawing produces a fiber that is pliable, elastic, flexible, and tough. Fibers can also be produced by extrusion, in which small granules of polymer are melted and forced through a nozzle. The plastic mass is shaped by being forced through a die as it emerges. The result is a continuous length of fiber, the same shape all the way through. Dacron (Terylene) fibers can be produced in this way. Extrusion is also used to produce sheets, films, and various types of tubes and pipes. Extruded objects usually require further processing before they can be considered finished goods.

Injection molding

Injection molding can be used to produce a wide variety of shapes with great accuracy. In an injection molding machine, an injection unit, consisting of an extruder with a screw that can be moved backward and forward, melts the feed material as the screw moves backward, then forces the material out into the mold as the screw is driven forward. The mold is opened to remove the finished item. Goods produced in this way generally do not need further processing.

To make hollow objects, such as bottles, cans, or other containers, extrusion blow molding is used. In this process, an extruder forces a plastic tube vertically downward between the two halves of an open two-part mold. After the mold is closed and sealed, compressed air is blown into the tube to force the soft

Dacron or Terylene

Trade names for a type of polyester called polyethylene terephthalate, or PET. Dacron or Terylene fibers are often added into natural fabrics such as cotton to improve properties such as crease resistance. PET is also used for making products such as soda bottles.

PVC (polyvinyl chloride) being calendered between pairs of rollers to produce thin sheets. The temperature of the rollers and the pressure they exert affect the properties of the PVC sheet that is produced.

plastic against the sides of the mold and form the desired hollow shape.

Calendering and foaming

Calendering is used to produce semifinished goods, such as coverings, flooring, and plastic sheets for use as wrappings. Polyvinyl chloride is often processed in this way to produce PVC sheeting and to coat fabrics. Calendering machines work on a similar principle to old-fashioned kitchen mangles. A melted mass of polymer is passed over and through a series of heated rollers to form a sheet.

Many polymers, such as polystyrene, polyethylene, and PVC, can be expanded or foamed to reduce their density. In foaming, a gas is included in the polymer structure. This can be done by mixing compressed air or gas into the melted polymer mass. Another method involves adding a blowing agent such as sodium bicarbonate to the plastic raw materials. When the hot melt is formed, the sodium bicarbonate decomposes to give off carbon dioxide gas, which forms bubbles in the foam. Expanded polymers can be made into products ranging from egg boxes and drinking cups to sponges and steering wheels for cars, by methods such as injection molding, extrusion, and calendering.

Using Plastics

A wide range of properties can be designed into polymers, with the result that polymers are in use almost everywhere. Tough plastics are replacing ceramics and cast iron. Polymer-based synthetic fibers are replacing wool and silk to make strong carpets, and replacing other natural fibers to make clothing that lasts longer and needs no ironing.

Major differences in the physical properties of polymers result from the types of intermolecular forces between chains; they also account for the great differences between hard, rigid thermosetting plastics and thermoplastic polymers, which can be shaped again and again because they become soft and moldable when heated, without undergoing any chemical change.

One of the best known thermosetting plastics, and the first to be invented, is Bakelite. It is produced using a condensation reaction involving phenol (C_6H_5OH) and methanal (formaldehyde, HCHO). During curing at high temperatures, strong covalent bonds form between the polymer chains and result in a strong, rigid material. Bakelite is a good electrical insulator and can be machined and dyed. It is still commonly used for distributor caps on cars.

Arrangements of monomers

Differences in the nature of the polymer chains themselves also play an important role in controlling physical properties. For example, the monomer propene (C_3H_6) can be arranged in three different ways in the plastic polypropylene to produce three forms of the polymer, each with different physical properties.

In one form, the polymer chain contains monomers arranged in a regular sequence. This results in a

Curriculum Context

For many curricula, students should understand how the presence of single, double, and triple bonds determines the geometry of carbon-based molecules. These molecules include complex biological molecules (e.g. proteins) and many manufactured polymers used in daily life (e.g. polyester, nylon, and polypropylene).

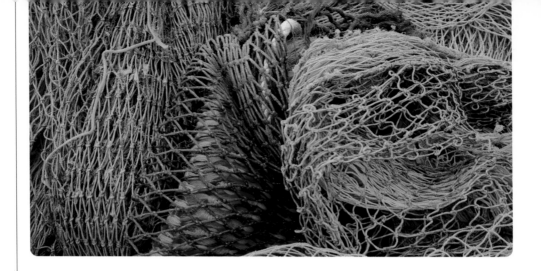

Nylon was originally developed as a synthetic alternative to silk. It was first used in stockings and other clothing. Today, nylon is still used for clothing, and it has almost completely replaced traditional materials for ropes and for fishing nets.

polymer with good mechanical strength. In a second form, the chains are compressed to form a crystalline polymer that is used to make blow-molded items such as bottles, and for packaging film. In atactic polypropylene, the chains are disordered. This results in a pliable material that is slightly tacky to the touch. It is used in backings for carpet tiles, and mixed with bitumen for use on roads and roofs.

Branching

Branching in the polymer chain is another important variable. The familiar thermoplastic polymer polyethene (polyethylene, best known as polythene) is available in low- and high-density forms whose differing physical properties relate to the amount of branching in the polymer chain. Low-density polyethylene (LDPE), which is formed during a high-pressure polymerization process, is made up of highly branched chains. In contrast, the polymer chains in high-density polyethylene (HDPE), produced using a low-pressure polymerization process, are generally linear and contain few branches.

The branching LDPE chains cannot be tightly packed. As a result, LDPE is relatively soft and has a low level of crystallinity and density. The linear HDPE chains can be closely packed. HDPE is harder than LDPE, and has a higher crystallinity and higher density. It is stronger and less easily deformed by heat than LDPE, and can be easily molded into complicated shapes. It is used to make vehicle fuel tanks, water tanks, and piping.

Nylon

Polymers can also be formed into fibers, which can then be woven or knitted to form a fabric. The first completely synthetic fiber was nylon, a polyamide incorporating the monomers diaminohexane and adipic acid. Nylon is characterized by high strength, elasticity, toughness, abrasive resistance, and low-temperature flexibility. It is also generally resistant to most solvents, acids, bases, and outdoor weathering.

Nylon fibers are produced by cold drawing, a process that causes all the polymer chains to become oriented along the length of the fiber. Nylon fibers are widely used in textiles, including stockings, as well as for tire cord, rope, threads, and belts.

Polyesters and aramids

Cold drawing also provided the breakthrough needed to produce polyester fibers from polyester, a polymer formed by a condensation reaction between polyhydric alcohols and organic acids. Polyester fibers are strong and resistant to heat, and when mixed with cotton fibers they make cool, comfortable clothing that does not crease easily.

Amides, the monomer units in nylon, provided the basis for the development of polyaramids, which make up tough, fire-resistant materials such as Kevlar. This low-density fiber is, weight for weight, nearly five times as strong as steel. The strength comes from the arrangement of the polymer chains, which lie parallel to one another and are held together in sheets by hydrogen bonds. The sheets are stacked regularly around the fiber axis in a very well-ordered structure.

Adipic acid
A six-carbon dicarboxylic acid, formula $HOOC- (CH_2)_4-COOH$.

Polyhydric alcohol
An alcohol containing multiple hydroxyl $(-OH)$ groups.

Amide
An organic compound in which a carbonyl group is linked to a nitrogen, with the general formula $R-CHO-NR'-R'$, where R is any functional group.

Recycling Polymers

Plastic garbage is a common but unwelcome sight around the world. Even the open ocean is not free of it, and plastic trash from ships, yachts, and oil rigs spoils the beauty of beaches around the world. Often, plastics are considered undesirable when compared to more "natural" materials such as paper.

Environmental costs

A study carried out by the German Federal Office analyzed the environmental cost of using plastic carrier bags as compared with paper ones. The study showed that plastic bags are not only cheaper, but actually more environmentally friendly. Their production creates less than half the pollution of paper bags, uses less energy, and produces 200 times less waste water.

Although plastic has been shown to be less harmful to the environment than was once thought, the sheer volume of plastic waste poses another problem, and the best method of disposal is not a straightforward choice. More than 85 percent of plastic waste is currently buried in landfill sites or burned. Burning has some advantages, because plastic waste contains energy that can be reused. However, burning must be carefully controlled to avoid giving off dangerous pollutants such as dioxins.

Dioxins

Heterocyclic organic compounds that are released into the air as a result of many industrial processes. Studies have shown that dioxins can be toxic at very low concentrations.

Recycling

Degradable plastics—which break down into smaller molecules after use—are one possible way to solve the trash problem. Alternatively, some people believe that recycling plastics is the answer. Unlike paper and glass, plastic waste is difficult to recycle because it is not uniform—there are many different types of plastic in circulation. But some plastics, such as polyethylene terephthalate (PET), which is used to make bottles and jars, show good potential for recycling.

Hydrolysis

Some polymers, such as polyurethane foam, can be hydrolyzed using high-pressure steam to break them down into their component materials, which can then be reused. Other polymers can be reduced to simple hydrocarbons by means of pyrolysis—"burning" or thermal decomposition in the absence of air.

Degradable plastics

There are two main ways of degrading plastics to help them rot away: biodegradation and photodegradation. Biodegradable plastics (like the polyhydroxybutyrate manufactured under the tradename Biopol) are made out of materials that microbes will digest. Some biodegradable plastics include the biological polymer starch, which microbes can digest.

Photodegradable plastics contain molecules whose bonds are broken by exposure to sunlight. Some incorporate a carbonyl unit ($-C=O$), which absorbs energy from photons of light. When the energy builds up, it fractures the polymer chain.

Pyrolysis (heating in the absence of oxygen) can be used to recycle mixed plastics. It is commonly carried out at temperatures between 752°F (400°C) and 1,472°F (800°C). About half the gases produced are recycled to fuel the process. The remaining gases, along with the liquid hydrocarbons the process produces, can be separated in a fractional distillation column.

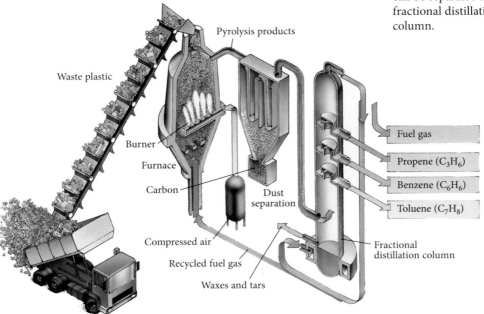

Waste plastic

Pyrolysis products

Burner

Furnace

Carbon

Compressed air

Recycled fuel gas

Waxes and tars

Dust separation

Fuel gas

Propene (C_3H_6)

Benzene (C_6H_6)

Toluene (C_7H_8)

Fractional distillation column

Vital Raw Materials

Only six principal types of molecules form the basis of all living organisms. These key molecules are made up from just a handful of chemical elements: hydrogen, oxygen, carbon, nitrogen, phosphorus, and sulfur.

Biochemistry is the basis of life. Chemical reactions go on continuously in all organisms. If these reactions are disturbed by the activities of microorganisms such as bacteria and viruses, which cause illness, it may be possible to use chemistry to correct them.

Food provides energy and essential nutrients. Before any of the important chemicals in food can be used by the body, the food must be broken down. Food is physically broken down by chewing and by churning in the stomach, and chemically broken up by enzymes—proteins that act as catalysts in living systems.

Respiration

Like hydrocarbons and other fuels, food contains stored chemical energy. But whereas energy is released from hydrocarbons very quickly during combustion, energy is released in a controlled way from food during a different type of oxidation process, known as respiration. This is a complex sequence of chemical reactions in which sugars are broken down by reaction with oxygen. As with combustion, the products of respiration are energy, carbon dioxide, and water. Some of the energy is released as heat, and some is stored in adenosine triphosphate (ATP) molecules, which are broken down into adenosine diphosphate (ADP) to release stored energy as needed.

Essential nutrients

In order to stay healthy, people must include in their diet vitamins, mineral salts, fiber, water, lipids (fats and oils), carbohydrates, and proteins. Vitamins and

Curriculum Context

For many curricula, students should know that respiration is a process in which energy is released when chemical compounds react with oxygen. In respiration, sugars are broken down to produce useful chemical energy.

Vitamins

Simple chemicals found in food that are essential in small amounts for correct body functioning.

minerals protect the body from disease. They also act to help the body make use of other nutrients. Minerals also provide important elements needed to make more complicated molecules. Fiber helps the body to dispose of waste material. Water, which makes up roughly 75 percent of the human body, provides the essential solvent in which most biochemical processes take place.

Lipids and carbohydrates

Lipids (fats and oils) are important sources of stored energy. Lipids comprise a glycerol molecule ($CH_2OH.CHOH.CH_2OH$) with three long fatty acid chains attached. Each of the fatty acid chains is mainly hydrocarbon. The glycerol and fatty acids are released during digestion, and recombine as new fats that can be stored in various body tissues.

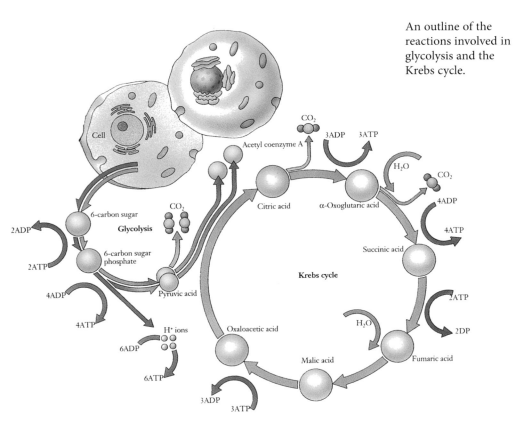

An outline of the reactions involved in glycolysis and the Krebs cycle.

Carbohydrates, such as starches and sugars, are made up of carbon, hydrogen, and oxygen. These large molecules are broken down to form smaller sugars such as glucose ($C_6H_{12}O_6$) and its structural isomer, fructose. Glucose and other sugars are the main energy source for the body.

Glycolysis and the Krebs Cycle

Glucose is broken down via a series of reactions that produce molecules of ATP (adenosine triphosphate). The first step in respiration is glycolysis. During this process, enzymes catalyze the breakdown of glucose into molecules of pyruvic acid. The pyruvic acid feeds into a complex cycle of enzyme-controlled reactions known as the Krebs or citric acid cycle.

Various chemical reactions in glycolysis and the Krebs cycle produce energy. This energy is captured, either directly or indirectly, in molecules of ATP. ATP is the energy currency of the cell. When it is converted to ADP (adenosine diphosphate), by the removal of a phosphate group, energy is released. This energy can be used to drive other biochemical reactions in the cell.

Curriculum Context

For most curricula, students should know that proteins are large, single-stranded polymers often made up of thousands of relatively small subunits called amino acids.

Proteins

Proteins are the building blocks of cells and tissues, and need to be continuously replaced. They are made up of amino acids—smaller molecules that include an amino group ($-NH_2$) and a carboxylic acid ($-COOH$). There are about 20 amino acids, which can be combined to make up thousands of different proteins. Proteins can contain more than 4,000 amino acid units. The proteins in food are broken down during digestion into their basic amino acids, which can join together to make different proteins. One amino acid can be converted into another, and some can be made from carbohydrates. But there are ten essential amino acids that cannot be manufactured by the body, and these must be taken in as food.

Living Chemistry

All living things are chemical machines. Chemical reactions within the body provide organisms with energy, get rid of waste products, and keep them healthy. Almost all biological processes rely on catalysts in the form of proteins known as enzymes.

Enzymes

Enzymes are highly specialized proteins that regulate metabolism (the thousands of chemical processes that occur in a cell or organism). They act as organic catalysts that speed up chemical reactions in living cells. Without their catalyzing power, many biochemical reactions would proceed too slowly to sustain life. There are thousands of different enzymes. Most work during metabolism as part of a chain reaction, or catalytic cycle. In general, the product of one enzyme-induced reaction becomes the reactant for the next.

The action of enzymes is very specific. Most enzymes are involved in just one chemical reaction. Their structure explains why. Like all proteins, they are composed of chains of amino acids. This protein chain folds itself into a specific shape, which is held together by weak dipole–dipole interactions and hydrogen bonds. The surface of the enzyme contains specially shaped areas called active sites, in which catalysis takes place. An enzyme's active site is carefully shaped to fit the reactants for a particular reaction, in the same way that a lock is designed to accept a particular key.

An enzyme becomes inactive if its shape is changed. This inactivation process is called denaturation. An enzyme may be denatured by changes in temperature, which cause the molecules to vibrate more vigorously and thus break the weak interactions that hold the chain in shape. Changes in pH can interfere with the ionic interactions within the protein chain, and this can also denature the enzyme.

Curriculum Context

For most curricula, students should know that living systems speed up life-dependent reactions with biological catalysts called enzymes.

Curriculum Context

For many curricula, students should know that hormones act as chemical messengers, affecting the activity of neighboring cells or other target organs.

Hormones

Hormones are the chemical messengers used by the endocrine system in animals to control and regulate body chemistry. In plants, phytohormones do a similar job. Hormones are produced in one part of the body, and then transported—usually via the bloodstream—to a target cell in another part, where they act by regulating preexisting processes.

There are three main types of hormones. Peptide, polypeptide, and protein hormones such as somato-tropin, the growth hormone, are formed from chains of

A computer model of one subunit of the protein hemoglobin. The complete protein has four subunits. The spirals and straighter sections show the shape of the protein chain. Hemoglobin is not strictly an enzyme. However, like an enzyme it has an active site (center), where oxygen binds to the heme molecule.

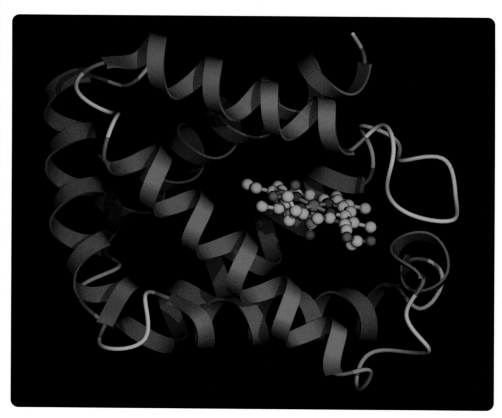

amino acids of various lengths. Hormones such as epinephrine (adrenaline), which prepares the body for fast action in an emergency, are based on amino acid derivatives known as amides, which are organic compounds in which one or more of the hydrogen atoms in ammonia (NH_3) have been replaced by an acyl group (–RCO). Steroid hormones, such as the sex hormones, are based on the linked benzene rings that make up the molecule cholesterol.

Hormone actions

Hormones perform crucial roles. For example, the polypeptide hormones insulin and glucagon, and the amide-based hormone epinephrine, work together to control glucose levels in the blood. Glucose is stored, mainly in the liver and muscles, as the carbohydrate glycogen. When blood glucose levels fall below normal, glucagon and epinephrine are released into the bloodstream. They act to increase the rate at which glycogen is converted to glucose. This leads to an increase in blood glucose levels.

If blood glucose levels become too high, insulin is released. It stimulates the liver and muscles to convert blood glucose into glycogen, so that glucose levels fall. In this feedback loop, the amounts of insulin and glucagon produced are determined by the level of glucose in the blood, while the overall level of glucose is determined by the balance between these two hormones.

Diabetic people do not produce enough insulin, and so are unable to take in glucose from their blood. Diabetes has many serious symptoms and can lead to death if not treated.

Polypeptide
A single protein chain, usually a relatively short one.

Chemistry of Food

Like everything else around us, food is made up of various chemicals. These include the energy- and fiber-producing substances, carbohydrates, proteins, and fats, as well as essential vitamins and minerals.

Isomers

Molecules that have the same empirical formula (i.e. the same numbers of the same atoms) but arranged in different ways.

Curriculum Context

For most curricula, students should know that respiration is a process in which sugars are broken down to produce useful chemical energy.

RNA

Ribonucleic acid: a molecule similar to DNA, which has various roles in genetics.

Carbohydrates

Carbohydrates, such as cellulose, starches, and sugars, are made up of carbon, hydrogen, and oxygen. They are the main energy source for the body. During digestion, large carbohydrates are broken down to form sugars such as glucose ($C_6H_{12}O_6$) and its structural isomer, fructose. The sugars are broken down further to carbon dioxide and water, with the release of energy, in the process known as respiration (see page 86).

The glucose molecule can be represented as a six-membered ring containing five carbon atoms and one oxygen atom. Numbers of glucose units can join together (polymerize) to form the polysaccharides cellulose and starch. Humans cannot digest cellulose, but it does provide the main food source for plant-eating animals. Humans can digest starch from cereals and root vegetables, which is broken down into its component glucose units. These can be combined again in the liver to form the poly-saccharide glycogen, which is used as an energy store. The molecules of the disaccharides lactose (from milk), maltose (from barley), and sucrose (from sugar cane or sugar beet) also include one glucose unit.

Some sugars have a five-membered ring (four carbon atoms and one oxygen atom). They include ribose and deoxyribose, the sugars found in DNA and RNA. These sugars are found in all animal and plant cells. Another sugar with a five-membered ring is ribulose diphosphate. This is an important sugar in the Calvin cycle—the process in which plants produce sugars.

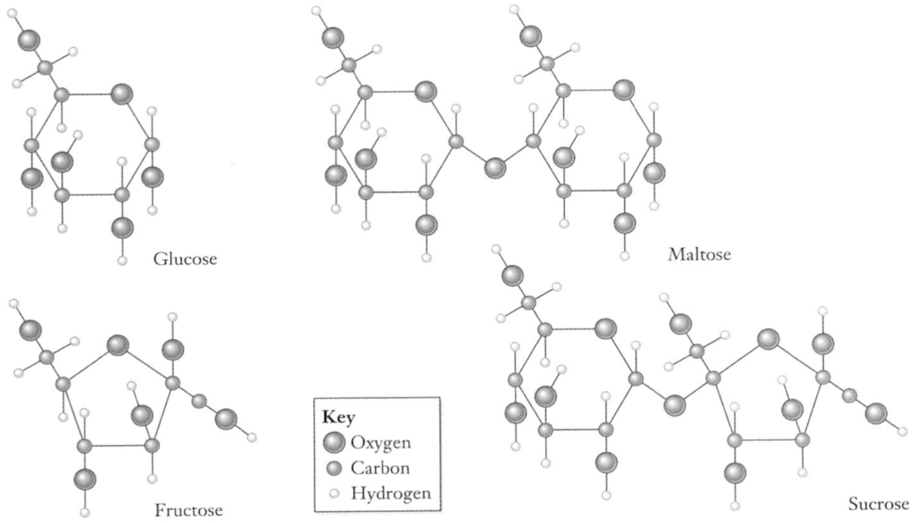

Glucose

Maltose

Key
- Oxygen
- Carbon
- Hydrogen

Fructose

Sucrose

Lipids

Fats and oils (lipids)—which are made up only of carbon, hydrogen, and oxygen—are important sources of stored energy. Lipids consist of a "stem" of glycerol with three fatty acid molecules attached. Each of the fatty acids is made up of a long chain of carbon atoms, which have mainly hydrogen atoms attached to them. Humans who eat meat derive much of their dietary fat from this source, although vegetarians have to rely on plant sources, such as nuts. The glycerol and fatty acids are released during digestion and recombine to form new fats, which can be stored in various body tissues.

Proteins

Proteins are the building blocks of cells and tissues. For this reason, proteins need to be continuously replaced in the body. They are made up of amino acids—smaller molecules in which an amino group ($-NH_2$), a carboxylic acid (with the group –COOH), and a side chain are attached to a carbon atom.

There are about 20 amino acids, which can be combined to make up thousands of different proteins. Proteins can contain more than 4,000 amino acid units.

Glucose and fructose are known as monosaccharides—they consist of a single sugar unit. Sucrose (formed from glucose and fructose) and maltose (formed from two glucoses) are disaccharides—they comprise two sugar units. Larger carbohydrates such as cellulose and starch are known as polysaccharides—they have many sugar units.

About half of the amino acids we require are produced by cells within the body. But ten of them, the so-called essential amino acids, cannot be synthesized in cells and so have to be provided in the food we eat. Plants, on the other hand, can synthesize all the amino acids they need as long as they have a supply of nitrogen.

Vitamins and minerals

Vitamins are nutrients that are essential in small quantities. There are up to 14 vitamins, which can be divided into fat-soluble and water-soluble vitamins. The chief fat-soluble vitamins are vitamins A (retinol), D (calciferol), E (tocopherol), and K (phylloquinone). Vitamin A is needed for the maintenance of good vision (deficiency causes night blindness), and vitamin D is needed to maintain healthy bones in growing children (deficiency causes rickets). Vitamin E seems to be associated with liver and muscle function and with fertility, while vitamin K is necessary for the functioning of the blood-clotting mechanism (a deficiency leads to copious bleeding in the tissues).

The water-soluble group includes the nine members of the vitamin B complex and vitamin C. The B vitamins include B1 (thiamine), B2 (riboflavin), B6 (pyroxine), and B12 (cobalamin). Their main purpose in the body is to act as components of coenzymes. Vitamin C (ascorbic acid) has many functions. One important function is that it is needed for the maintenance of healthy connective tissue (deficiency causes scurvy).

Food also provides the body with trace quantities of various inorganic minerals. These include, in order of concentration in the body, calcium and phosphorus, for bones and teeth; sulfur, part of the vitamins biotin and thiamine; potassium and sodium, for the functioning of nerves and muscles; and iron, for the formation of hemoglobin in the blood.

Coenzyme

Small, non-protein molecules that need to be present for some enzymes to work properly. Adenosine triphosphate (ADP) is one example of a coenzyme. Metal ions can also be coenzymes.

Scurvy

A disease caused by lack of vitamin C that produces livid spots on the skin, spongy gums, loosening of the teeth, and bleeding into the skin.

Chemicals in Agriculture

Every year the agriculture industry uses millions of tons of artificial fertilizers, to improve the fertility of soil and replenish elements removed from it by previously grown crops. Farmers also use tons of pesticides to kill unwanted insects and weeds.

Fertilizers

The main elements required by plants are phosphorus (P), potassium (K), and nitrogen (N). The main phosphorus-containing fertilizers are phosphates, manufactured from the mineral rock phosphate or apatite. This mineral may be treated with concentrated sulfuric acid to produce superphosphate, which was first made in the early 1800s from bones.

Potassium fertilizers include three salts: potassium chloride, potassium nitrate, and potassium sulfate. Most modern nitrogen fertilizers are made from ammonia, produced by the Haber process (see page 44), and can be applied to the land directly. Alternatively, the ammonia is made into salts such as ammonium sulfate and ammonium phosphate (which also provides phosphorus).

Herbicides and fungicides

Farmers use herbicides for killing plants that are considered weeds. Selective weedkillers, which attack particular species of weeds, include diquat and paraquat, which work through the leaves. Systemic herbicides such as 2,4-D and picrolam are applied to the soil, where they are picked up by the roots and distributed throughout the plant to kill it.

Fungicides are used to kill fungi and molds. Traditional fungicides include sulfur and compounds of cadmium, copper, and mercury. Modern systemic fungicides are synthetic organic compounds. Examples include substituted benzenes such as Dicloran.

> **Apatite**
>
> A group of rock types containing calcium, phosphate ($PO_4{}^{3-}$), and other ions, such as fluoride (F^-) and hydroxide (OH^-).

Insecticides

One way of classifying insecticides is by their modes of action. Contact poisons, which attack through the insect's cuticle, include natural substances like nicotine and pyrethrum (obtained from certain chrysanthemum flowers) and synthetic substances such as organochlorine compounds (aldrin, BHC, DDT, and dieldrin) and the much more toxic organophosphates (malathion, parathion). Stomach poisons include inorganic compounds containing arsenic or fluorine. The fairly new carbamate insecticides are based on carbamic acid and contain the organic group $-CONH_2$.

Pollution from agrochemicals

In Western nations in recent years, there has been concern that chemicals applied to the land and crops can result in pollution of water supplies; this concern has prompted a growing interest in returning to organic farming methods. However, many hungry people in underdeveloped countries think that the benefits from increased crop yields obtained using artificial fertilizers and pesticides far outweigh any possible problems arising from their use.

Insecticides and other pesticides (for example, fungicides) are generally applied to crops by spraying. There is some evidence that crop spraying can damage human health if a person is repeatedly exposed to it over a long period.

Medical Drugs

Diseases result from chemical changes that disrupt the life processes of organisms. Chemotherapy is a powerful tool to bring the chemical machine back into balance. Drugs play an important part in this chemical warfare. All drugs work by altering the biochemical processes in either the disease-causing organism or the organism affected by the disease.

Different types of drugs act in different ways to fight disease. Vaccines prevent illness by stimulating the body's immune system to develop antibodies. These are special proteins that attack and destroy disease-causing organisms. Other medicines affect the biochemical pathways in the attacking organism. This can involve, for example, blocking the action of enzymes and thus preventing biochemical reactions from going out of control; or preventing hormones from delivering their chemical messages, and thus blocking the response of a cell to a hormone. Antibiotics and sulfa drugs, both hailed as "wonder drugs" in their time, take this approach.

Curriculum Context

For many curricula, students should know the role of antibodies in the body's response to infection. They should also know how vaccination protects an individual from infectious diseases.

Antibiotics

Antibiotics are extracted from living microorganisms and selectively destroy disease-causing bacteria, often by inhibiting the action of important enzymes. Penicillin was originally extracted from molds (fungi). It stops the growth of new bacteria by inhibiting the action of an enzyme responsible for making the bacteria's cell walls. Sulfa drugs, in contrast, are produced in a test tube and inhibit bacteria from synthesizing folic acid, an essential nutrient. This prevents the bacteria from reproducing and gives the body's defense mechanisms a better chance of killing off the invaders. Sulfa drugs are harmless to humans because mammals cannot synthesize folic acid, and must include it in their diet.

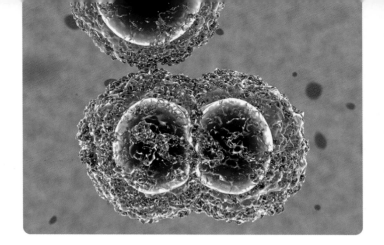

Some strains of bacteria, such as MRSA (methicillin-resistant *Staphylococcus aureus*), have developed resistance to all current antibiotics. MRSA infections are untreatable: patients must rely on their own immune system to fight off the illness.

Drug mechanisms

Like enzymes, drugs depend on a "lock and key" mechanism to work. The drug molecule must fit exactly into a receptor on the molecule whose chemistry it hopes to influence. It is also critical that the drug is delivered efficiently to the part of the body it is supposed to affect. For example, a pill must be designed so that the drug can reach its target area when absorbed from the digestive system. In some cases it is possible to attach a drug to an antibody, allowing the drug to target diseased cells directly. This approach is used to treat cancerous tumors.

Drug abuse

Not all drugs are medicines. Some can unbalance body chemistry and act as poisons. Drugs such as alcohol and cocaine depress the central nervous system by interfering with the activity of neurotransmitters and receptors on the nerve cells. These drugs can relieve pain and tension, but they also slow reaction times and impair judgment. When taken in large amounts, or in combination with other drugs, the effects can be fatal. Chronic overuse can cause physical deterioration, such as cirrhosis of the liver in alcoholics. Widespread misuse of barbiturates, another class of drugs that reduce the activity of the central nervous system, has made it necessary to restrict their use. In some countries they are now routinely prescribed only for epilepsy.

Neurotransmitters

Chemicals that act by crossing synapses (gaps between nerve cells) to transmit nerve impulses from cell to cell.

Finding New Drugs

By understanding the effects of diseases at the molecular level, chemists are able to search for—or to design and manufacture—specific substances to fight specific diseases. Some of the most widely used drugs were developed by extracting, refining, and purifying active ingredients derived from plants.

Aspirin, which is based on 2-hydroxybenzoic (or salicylic) acid—a compound found in the bark of the willow tree—is now synthetically produced by introducing an extra functional group into the phenol molecule to produce 2-ethanoylhydroxybenzoic acid. Digitalis is still made by refining an active compound found in a species of foxglove.

Drug screening
Random screening of alkaloids has resulted in the identification of many useful active compounds. The search for new drugs is concentrated in areas such as tropical rainforests, where there is a great diversity of plants whose properties have not yet been explored.

This approach led to the development of the drug captopril, which is widely used to treat high blood pressure. The inspiration for its development was the discovery that certain proteins in the venom of the Brazilian arrowhead viper (*Bothrops jararaca*) act as an inhibitor to block the action of an enzyme that is a key factor in raising blood pressure. By using the structure of the proteins in the venom as a starting point, chemists were able to synthesize a successful drug to lower blood pressure.

Chirality
As well as the composition of a drug, chemists also have to consider its shape and orientation. Many biological molecules are chiral—they exist in right- and

Alkaloid
Any naturally occurring, nitrogen-containing base. Many alkaloids are toxic to other organisms.

Plants continue to provide a more economical source of modern drugs than synthetic chemicals. Examples include the heart drug digitalis, which is still obtained from foxglove (1); caffeine, from the coffee plant (2); morphine, from the opium poppy (3); and atropine, from deadly nightshade (4).

left-handed forms, or isomers. Although they often have the same physical properties, and seem to behave chemically in the same way, they can have very different effects in the body. For example, right-handed amino acids taste sweet, whereas left-handed amino acids often taste bitter or have no taste at all.

Because it is expensive to separate the different isomers, many medicines are sold as racemic mixtures, in which there are equal numbers of left- and right-handed forms. Careful testing is necessary to make sure that they are not harmful. In the case of the drug thalidomide, the active isomer was a mild sedative, but when taken by pregnant women, the inactive isomer caused severe damage to their unborn children.

Testing a new drug

Today, with the help of powerful computer programs, chemists can use their knowledge of the chemical basis of disease to build up molecules and test their possible effects on the computer screen. They can, in effect, design drugs on screen. But in spite of the increasing success of computer-based drug design, and an understanding of the molecular basis of drug action and disease, finding, developing, and marketing a new drug is still very expensive and risky. Only about 1 in 10,000 of the compounds synthesized survives the rigorous testing to become a commercial drug.

Photosynthesis

Green plants use photosynthesis to capture energy radiated from the Sun. This sustains all life on Earth. In photosynthesis, water molecules are split and combined with carbon (derived from carbon dioxide in the atmosphere) to make the sugar glucose. The glucose is stored in the form of its polymer starch. It may be used to make the straight-chain polymer cellulose (the major supporting material in plant cell walls), or broken down by the plant during respiration to release energy. Most of the oxygen in the atmosphere that animals breathe is a byproduct of this reaction.

Biological pigments

The key molecules in all light-driven biochemical reactions are biological pigments, which capture the energy of light when incoming photons boost the electrons in some of the pigment molecule's atoms to a higher energy level. The key pigment is chlorophyll, a porphyrin that has a magnesium (Mg^{2+}) ion at its center. Several small side-chains, attached outside the porphyrin ring, alter the absorption properties in different types of chlorophyll.

Porphyrins are derivatives of porphin, a simpler purple compound (the name porphyrin is derived from the Greek work for purple). They are made up of pyrrole rings (see page 66), joined into a larger ring by methylene (−CH=) groups. Porphyrins readily lose their central hydrogen atoms to take on a negative charge. The charge is neutralized by positively-charged metal ions such as iron (Fe^{2+}), magnesium (Mg^{2+}), and cobalt (Co^{2+}), which fit into the center of the porphyrin molecule. Other well-known porphyrins include hemoglobin, the oxygen-carrying protein in blood (which has an Fe^{2+} ion at its center), and vitamin B12, which has key roles in the normal functioning of the brain and nervous system, and in the formation of blood (it has a Co^{2+} ion at its center).

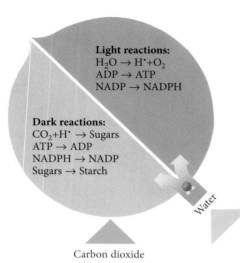

Light reactions:
$H_2O \rightarrow H^{\cdot} + O_2$
$ADP \rightarrow ATP$
$NADP \rightarrow NADPH$

Dark reactions:
$CO_2 + H^{\cdot} \rightarrow$ Sugars
$ATP \rightarrow ADP$
$NADPH \rightarrow NADP$
Sugars $\rightarrow$ Starch

Water

Carbon dioxide

▲ During the light and dark reactions of photosynthesis, the energy of light is captured and used to combine carbon dioxide and water to form sugars. (This process is called "fixing" carbon.) This conversion takes place in special organelles within plant cells, called chloroplasts.

▼ Nearly all photosynthesis takes place in a plant's leaves, in tight-packed palisade cells just beneath the upper leaf surface. Leaf veins bring water to the cells and take away sugars. Gas exchange takes place through pores called stomata on the leaf underside.

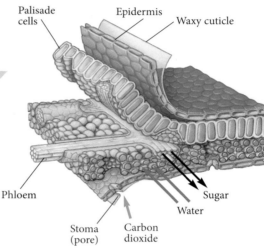

Palisade cells

Epidermis

Waxy cuticle

Phloem

Sugar

Water

Stoma (pore)

Carbon dioxide

Chlorophyll absorbs light energy in the red and blue region of the visible spectrum, and thus appears green. During photosynthesis, it transfers this light energy into chemical energy. This happens when the photons of light absorbed by the chlorophyll excite the electrons of the magnesium ions. The electrons are then channeled away through the carbon bond system of the porphyrin ring to fuel photosynthesis.

The light reactions

Photosynthesis involves three series of chemical events: the light reactions and the dark reactions, during which energy is captured and stored; and a series of reactions to replenish the pigments.

The light reactions can take place only in the presence of light, and occur on photosynthetic membranes in the chloroplasts of plants. During the reactions, a photon of light is captured by the chlorophyll molecule and excites an electron within the pigment. The excited electron travels along a series of electron-carrier molecules in the photosynthetic membrane to a transmembrane proton-pumping channel, where it induces a proton to cross the membrane. The proton later crosses back across the membrane, which drives the synthesis of the energy-carrying molecule adenosine triphosphate (ATP). In addition, a second type of energy-carrying molecule, nicotine adenine dinucleotide phosphate (NADP), is reduced to form the electron carrier NADPH.

The dark reactions

During the dark reactions, the energy from ATP and NADPH is used to make organic molecules from atmospheric carbon dioxide (CO_2) in a cycle of enzyme-catalyzed reactions known as carbon fixation.

During a third series of reactions, the electron that was stripped from the chlorophyll at the beginning of the light reactions is replaced. Without this, stage, the continuous removal of electrons from chlorophyll in photosynthesis would cause the pigment to become deficient in electrons and it would no longer be able to trap photon energy by electron excitation.

Curriculum Context

For most curricula, students need to know that plants and many microorganisms use solar energy to combine molecules of carbon dioxide and water into complex, energy-rich organic compounds and release oxygen to the environment.

Photosynthesis and Respiration

Photosynthesis and respiration are complementary processes. In photosynthesis, energy from the Sun is stored in sugars and other molecules. In respiration, sugars and other molecules are broken down to release energy.

Photosynthesis takes up carbon dioxide from the atmosphere, and releases oxygen as a waste product. Respiration takes up oxygen from the atmosphere, and produces carbon dioxide as a waste product.

Atmospheric Chemistry

The Earth is unique among the planets of the Solar System in having a chemically reactive atmosphere rich in oxygen. The chemistry of the atmosphere is a series of delicately balanced cycles involving many chemicals that interact closely. Photochemical reactions driven by sunlight play a key role.

The greenhouse effect

Without the atmosphere, the surface of the Earth would have an average temperature of around 0°F (−18°C). The greenhouse effect traps some of the energy of the Sun, raising the surface temperature to a more comfortable 59°F (15°C). This effect occurs because the "greenhouse gases" (mainly water vapor and carbon dioxide) trap radiated heat, which originates as high-energy short-wavelength radiation from the Sun. This energy is absorbed by the surface of the Earth, which, in turn, emits radiation of its own, but at much longer and lower-energy infrared wavelengths. Some of this radiated heat is trapped in the lower part of the atmosphere (the troposphere) by water vapor and carbon dioxide. The air near the surface of the Earth is warmed because the greenhouse gases do not allow all of the radiation to escape.

The burning of fossil fuels raises the levels of CO_2, upsets the natural balance of greenhouse gases in the atmosphere, and strengthens the greenhouse effect. Other gases released by human activities, including ozone, methane, nitrogen oxides, and chlorofluoro-carbons (CFCs), also contribute. This imbalance in the greenhouse effect is the main cause of climate change.

The ozone layer

CFCs also cause problems in the upper part of the atmosphere (the stratosphere). There, ozone (O_3) plays an important role in filtering out dangerous ultraviolet

Climate change

The continuing global increase in average temperatures that has been brought about by human activities, in particular the release of carbon dioxide into the atmosphere.

radiation from the Sun and preventing it from reaching the surface of the Earth.

Various chemicals known as free radicals, including chlorine (Cl) atoms, hydroxyl radicals (HO), and nitrogen oxides (NO_x), speed up the removal of ozone from the stratosphere by reacting with it. CFCs act as a vehicle to bring chlorine free radicals into the upper atmosphere. Because each chlorine atom can destroy roughly 100,000 molecules of ozone, the protective stratospheric ozone layer is under considerable threat.

Acid rain

Closer to Earth, nitrogen oxides, which include nitric oxide (NO) and nitrogen dioxide (NO_2), along with sulfur dioxide (SO_2), are all produced from the burning of fossil fuels. The sulfur dioxide reacts with rainwater to form sulfurous acid (H_2SO_3) and sulfuric acid (H_2SO_4). Nitrogen dioxide (NO_2) is oxidized and converted into nitric acid (HNO_3). Acid rain has been shown to damage plants and the ecology of lakes and watercourses.

In 1985, scientists at the British Antarctic Survey recognized a seasonal thinning, or hole, in the ozone layer over Antarctica. Measurements taken by satellites produced this image from the Total Ozone Mapping Spectrometer (TOMS). It shows the extent of the ozone hole in September 2003.

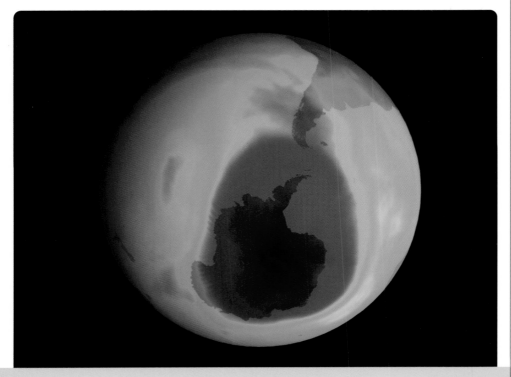

Glossary

Adipic acid A six-carbon dicarboxylic acid, formula HOOC–(CH$_2$)$_4$–COOH.

Aliphatic A term for carbon compounds that do not contain aromatic (benzene-like) rings.

Alkaloid Any naturally occurring, nitrogen-containing base. Many alkaloids are toxic to other organisms.

Alkanes Chemical compounds containing only carbon and hydrogen, bonded through single bonds.

Allotropy The property that some elements have of being able to take two or more different structural forms. Graphite and diamond, for example, are two allotropes of carbon.

Amalgam A compound formed by the reaction of a metal or some other substance with mercury.

Amide An organic compound in which a carbonyl group (=CO) is linked to a nitrogen, with the general formula R–CHO–NR'–R', where R is any functional group.

Amorphous Having no regular structure.

Apatite A group of rock types containing calcium, phosphate (PO$_4$$^{3-}$), and other ions, such as fluoride (F$^-$) and hydroxide (OH$^-$).

Atomic number The number of protons in the nucleus of an element. Carbon, for instance, has 12 protons in its nucleus (atomic number = 12).

Buckminster Fuller American architect and inventor who invented the geodesic dome—a hemispherical structure built from flat five-sided and six-sided panels.

Catalyst A substance that promotes or accelerates a chemical reaction without itself being permanently changed in the reaction.

Climate change The continuing global increase in average temperatures that has been brought about by human activities, in particular release of carbon dioxide into the atmosphere.

Coenzymes Small, non-protein molecules that need to be present for some enzymes to work properly. Adenosine triphosphate (ADP) is one example of a coenzyme. Metal ions can also be coenzymes.

Dioxins Heterocyclic organic compounds that are released into the air as a result of many industrial processes. Studies have shown that dioxins can be toxic at very low concentrations.

Dipole A weak positive–negative polarity in a covalent molecule.

Doping Intentionally introducing small amounts of impurities into a very pure material in order to change its physical properties.

Electrolysis The process that occurs when an electrolyte conducts electricity.

Electrolyte An ionic compound, such as an acid, alkali, or salt, which allows ions to flow through it. Electrolytes conduct electricity when they are melted or dissolved.

Evaporite A kind of sedimentary rock resulting from the evaporation of surface water, leaving behind a mineral deposit.

Fulminate A salt of fulminic acid (HCNO—an isomer of isocyanic acid).

Functional group A chemically reactive group of atoms, such as an alcohol (OH) or amine (NH$_3$) group, in an organic (carbon-based) compound.

Hydrocarbon A chemical compound that is made up only of carbon and hydrogen atoms. Fossil fuels are made up of hydrocarbons.

Hydrogen bond A weak bond formed between a polarized hydrogen atom and an electronegative atom (one that attracts electrons) such as oxygen.

Hydrolysis A chemical reaction in which a substance is split or broken down by reaction with water.

Ignition point The temperature at which a fuel will begin to burn.

Ion An atom that is positively or negatively charged.

Isomers Molecules that have the same empirical formula (i.e. the same numbers of the same atoms) but arranged in different ways.

Ligand A substance that can form a complex in which a number of ligand molecules bond to a central atom, often a metal.

Macromolecule A giant molecule formed by joining together multiple copies of one or more smaller molecules in single or branched chains.

Neurotransmitters Chemicals that act by crossing synapses (gaps between nerve cells) to transmit nerve impulses from cell to cell.

Noble gases Gases in Group VIII of the Periodic Table, all of which are chemically unreactive.

Nomenclature Any system devised for giving things names.

Organic solvent A solvent that dissolves organic compounds such as hydrocarbons, which are not soluble in water. Common organic solvents include ethyl alcohol (CH_3CH_2OH) and acetone (CH_3COCH_3).

Ozone layer A thin layer in the upper atmosphere that is rich in a variant form of oxygen (O_3) known as ozone. The ozone layer protects the Earth from harmful utraviolet and other radiation.

Photochemical reaction A chemical reaction in which the activation energy is supplied by light energy.

Plankton Marine organisms that are either microscopic or very small, which drift or weakly swim with the ocean currents rather than against them.

Polyhydric alcohol An alcohol containing multiple hydroxyl (–OH) groups.

Polypeptide A single protein chain, usually a relatively short one.

Radical In organic chemistry, radicals are groups of atoms that attach themselves to different compounds as if they were one element, and remain unchanged internally during chemical reactions.

Reactant An element or compound taking part in a chemical reaction.

RNA Ribonucleic acid: a molecule similar to DNA, which has various roles in genetics.

Scurvy A disease caused by lack of vitamin C that produces livid spots on the skin, spongy gums, loosening of the teeth, and bleeding into the skin.

Solute A solid or liquid dissolved in a solvent.

Solvent A liquid in which certain solids or liquids dissolve.

Surfactant A substance that reduces the surface tension of the water in which it is dissolved.

Suspension A mixture of fine, solid particles in a liquid, in which the solid particles remain suspended in the liquid rather than precipitating (sinking to the bottom).

Unsaturated compound An organic compound containing double or triple bonds, which make it more reactive than a saturated compound (one containing only single bonds).

Vitamins Simple chemicals found in food that are essential in small amounts for correct body functioning.

Volatile Any substance that evaporates at a low temperature to become a gas.

Yield A percentage calculated as the amount of product compared to the amount of feedstock used to produce that product.

Further Research

BOOKS

Atkins, Peter. W. *The Periodic Kingdom: A Journey into the Land of the Chemical Elements.* New York: Basic Books, 2008.

Cobb, Cathy, and Harold Goldwhite. *Creations of Fire: Chemistry's Lively History from Alchemy to the Atomic Age.* Cambridge, MA: Perseus Publishing, 1996.

Daintith, John (Editor). *A Dictionary of Chemistry.* New York: Oxford University Press, USA, 2008.

Emsley, John. *The Elements of Murder: A History of Poison.* New York: Oxford University Press, USA, 2006.

Faraday, Michael. *The Chemical History of a Candle.* New York: Dover Publications, 2002.

Lewis, Rob, and Wynne Evans. *Palgrave Foundations: Chemistry.* New York: Palgrave Macmillan, 2006.

Pople, Stephen, and Charles Taylor. *Science.* New York: Oxford University Press, USA, 2004.

Solway, Andrew. *Discovering Chemical Reactions: Gunpowder to Cold Fusion.* Oxford: Heinemann Library, 2007.

Wertheim, Jane, Chris Oxlade, and Corinne Stockley. *The Usborne Illustrated Dictionary of Chemistry.* London: Usborne Books, 2008.

Widmaier, Eric P. *The Stuff of Life: Profiles of Molecules That Make Us Tick.* New York: Palgrave Macmillan, 2003.

DVD

NOVA: *Fireworks!* WGBH Boston: PBS, 2003.

INTERNET RESOURCES

NOVA Interactives Archive: Chemistry. Archives of interesting features from the NOVA TV programs that relate to chemistry. They include the anatomy of a firework, how to build a steroid, and an interactive laboratory about fire.
www.pbs.org/wgbh/nova/hotscience/int_chem.html

The Nobel Prize in Chemistry. The Nobel Prize website includes biographical information on the many winners of the Chemistry prize, including Marie Curie and her daughter Irene Joliot-Curie, Ernest Rutherford, and Fritz Haber.
nobelprize.org/nobel_prizes/chemistry

Pharmaceutical Achievers. Read some interesting stories about the discoverers of some of our most important medicines.
www.chemheritage.org/EducationalServices/pharm/pa/topics.htm

The Future's Plastic. An excellent website based on a BBC radio program about plastics and their history.
www.bbc.co.uk/radio4/science/futuresplastic.shtml

Science Museum: Chemistry and Materials. Interesting features on aspects of chemistry, including the history of atomic research, exploring the world of materials, and the first hundred years of plastics.
www.sciencemuseum.org.uk/visitmuseum/subjects/chemistry_and_materials.aspx

Webelements. The best-known Periodic Table on the internet, with useful information about every element.
www.webelements.com/

Discovery and Naming of the Chemical Elements. Which element was first discovered on the Sun? Which elements were named for the seven ancient "planets"? You can find the answers to these and many other questions on this fact-packed website.
homepage.mac.com/dtrapp/Elements/elements.html

The Periodic Table of Comic Books. "He's changing himself—into pure carbon—a diamond!" A fun website with sections of comic strips about the different elements.
www.uky.edu/Projects/Chemcomics/index.html

The Naked Scientists. A website covering all aspects of science, including physics, based on a series of radio programs created by a group of Cambridge University physicians and researchers.
www.thenakedscientists.com

New Scientist. The latest news and limited access to articles from *New Scientist* magazine.
www.newscientist.com

Scientific American. Breaking news and some access to features and articles from *Scientific American* magazine.
www.sciam.com

Index

Page numbers in **bold** refer to full articles; page numbers in *italic* refer to illustrations and captions.

F

fats and oils 11, 45, 50, 52, 61, 68, 93
fatty acid 50, 69, 87, 93
feedback 91
feedstock 42, 58
fermentation 43, 60
fertilizer 95
fiber 79, 86, 87
fiberglass 71
film, photographic 36, 47
filtration 49
fire break 30
fire extinguisher 28, 29, 30
fire triangle 28
firecracker 31
firefighting 29, 30
"fixing" nitrogen 37
flash point (ignition point) 27
flue gases 37
fluorine 15
food 25, 86, **92–94**
formaldehyde resin 76
formula, chemical 16, **21–22**
fossil fuels 57, 104, 105
fractional distillation 58, 59, 85
free radical 35, 105
fuel **25–27**, 28, 31, 53, 55, 69
functional group 21
fungicide 95
furan ring 65–66

G

gas (natural) 42, 55, 57
gasoline 26, 27, 59
glass manufacture 45, 46
glucagon 91
glucose 21, 41, 88, 92, 101
glycerol 87, 93
glycogen 91, 92
glycolysis 87, 88
graphite 16, 40
greenhouse effect 104
guanine 67
guncotton 32
gunpowder 31

H

Haber process 44, 45, 95
halogen 8, 18, 36
halogenated hydrocarbons 30
HDPE 82
hemoglobin 66, 90, 94, 102
herbicide 95
heterocyclic compounds **65–67**, 66
homologous series 54

hormone 63, 89, 91, 97
hydrocarbon 18, 25, 50, 54, 55, 56, **57–59**, 60, 61, **68–69**, 74, 75, 86
hydrochloric acid (HCl) 23, 34
hydrogen (H) 12, 14–15, 18, 20, 21, 25, 34–35, 44, 57, 60, 69, 70, 87, 93
hydrogen bond 12, 17, 83
hydrogenation 68, 69, 69
hydrolysis 85
hydrophobic 50, 52, 71
hydroquinone 36
hydroxyl group (–OH) 60

I

ignition point (flash point) 27
imidazole 67
immune system 97, 98
indicator 24
infrared (IR) 104
insecticide 96
insulin 91
ionic bond 14
ions 11, 12, 23, 24, 36, 41, 49, 50, 59
iron (Fe) 11, 67, 94
isomer 13, 54, 100
isoprene 74
isotope 9
IUPAC (International Union of Pure and Applied Chemistry) 21

K

kerosene 59
Kevlar 83
kieselguhr 32
Krebs cycle 87, 88

L

landfill site 84
latex 70, 74
lattice 15
LDPE 82, 83
lead–acid battery 49
Lewis diagram 22
ligand 16
light 19, 20, 34–36, 47, 51, 57, 101–103
lipid 86, 87–88, 93
litmus 24
lock and key mechanism 89, 98
lye 50

M

magnesium (Mg) 11, 50, 51, 101, 102
malathion 96
margarine 11
melting point 16, 54, 71, 74
Mendeleev, Dmitri 7
mercury (Hg) 40
metabolism 89
metallic bond 14
metalloids 7
metals 7, 56
methanal (CH$_2$O, formaldehyde) 61, 81
methane (CH$_4$) 54, 55, 104
micelle 52
microorganisms 86
mineral 7, 42, 86, 87, 94, 95
mixture **10–12**
molding 79–80, 82
molecule 10, 11, 12, 13, 17, 21, 22, 31, 53, 54, 55, 60, 62, 72, 73, 77, 86, 87, 90, 2, 98, 100, 105
monomer 70, 72, 75, 76, 77, 81
morphine 100
MRSA 98

N

NADP/NADPH (nicotinamide adenine dinucleotide phosphate) 103
nanotube 17
naphtha 59, 75
naphthalene 64
negative charge 51
neoprene 75
neutralization 19, 23
neutron 6, 9, 13
nitric acid 32, 33, 73, 105
nitrocellulose 32–33, 32, 73
nitrogen (N) 8, 20, 25, 27, 37, 38, 44, 65, 66, 67, 70, 77, 94, 95, 99, 104, 105
nitrogen oxides 27, 37, 104, 105
nitroglycerin 31–32
Nobel, Alfred 32
noble gas 8, 13
nonmetals 7, 8
nylon 79, 82, 83

O

octane rating 14
oil (petroleum) 13, 42, 50, 57, 58, 69, 74, 75
oleum 48
optical brightener 51–52